The Public Pol

MW01491718

Fully revised for a second edition, this essential guide provides a concise and accessible overview of the public policy process: agenda-setting, policy formulation, decision-making, implementation, and evaluation.

The book provides an introduction to the key policy functions, the challenges they entail, and how the challenges may be addressed by policy actors. Written from a comparative perspective, the authors include examples from a diverse range of countries at different stages of development, highlighting key principles and practices through which policy actors can effectively manage their policy processes and outcomes.

Key features of the second edition:

- fully updated and revised content throughout;
- expanded references and further reading;
- more guidance towards understanding the key concepts in public policy.

This important tool offers students of public policy and policy practitioners guidance on how to make, implement, and evaluate public policies in ways that improve citizens' lives.

Xun Wu is Professor in the Division of Public Policy and the Division of Social Science at the Hong Kong University of Science and Technology.

M. Ramesh is UNESCO Chair of Social Policy Design in Asia at the Lee Kuan Yew School of Public Policy at the National University of Singapore.

Michael Howlett is Burnaby Mountain Professor in the Department of Political Science at the Simon Fraser University, Canada, and Yong Pung How Chair Professor at the Lee Kuan Yew School of Public Policy at the National University of Singapore.

Scott A. Fritzen is Associate Professor at the Daniel J. Evans School of Public Policy and Governance at the University of Washington.

Routledge Textbooks in Policy Studies

This series provides high-quality textbooks and teaching materials for upper-level courses on all aspects of public policy as well as policy analysis, design, practice and evaluation. Each text is authored or edited by a leading scholar in the field and aims both to survey established areas and present the latest thinking on emerging topics.

The Public Policy Primer
Managing the Policy Process
Xun Wu, M Ramesh, Michael Howlett and Scott Fritzen

Designing Public Policies
Principles and Instruments
Michael Howlett

Making Policy Work
Peter John

Analyzing Public Policy, 2nd Edition
Peter John

Public Policy and Private Interest
Ideas, Self-Interest and Ethics in Public Policy
J.A. Chandler

The Public Policy Primer
Managing the Policy Process, 2nd Edition
Xun Wu, M. Ramesh, Michael Howlett and Scott A. Fritzen

The Public Policy Primer

Managing the Policy Process

Second Edition

**Xun Wu, M. Ramesh,
Michael Howlett, and
Scott A. Fritzen**

Routledge
Taylor & Francis Group

LONDON AND NEW YORK

Second edition published 2018
by Routledge
2 Park Square, Milton Park, Abingdon, Oxon OX14 4RN

and by Routledge
711 Third Avenue, New York, NY 10017

Routledge is an imprint of the Taylor & Francis Group, an informa business

© 2018 Xun Wu, M. Ramesh, Michael Howlett, and Scott A. Fritzen

The right of Xun Wu, M. Ramesh, Michael Howlett, and Scott A. Fritzen
to be identified as authors of this work has been asserted by them in
accordance with sections 77 and 78 of the Copyright, Designs and Patents
Act 1988.

All rights reserved. No part of this book may be reprinted or reproduced
or utilised in any form or by any electronic, mechanical, or other means,
now known or hereafter invented, including photocopying and recording,
or in any information storage or retrieval system, without permission in
writing from the publishers.

Trademark notice: Product or corporate names may be trademarks or
registered trademarks, and are used only for identification and explanation
without intent to infringe.

First edition published by Routledge 2010

British Library Cataloguing-in-Publication Data
A catalogue record for this book is available from the British Library

Library of Congress Cataloging-in-Publication Data
A catalog record for this book has been requested

ISBN: 978-1-138-65153-1 (hbk)
ISBN: 978-1-138-65154-8 (pbk)
ISBN: 978-1-315-62475-4 (ebk)

Typeset in Times New Roman
by Florence Production Ltd, Stoodleigh, Devon, UK

MIX
Paper from
responsible sources
FSC C013985

Printed in the United Kingdom
by Henry Ling Limited

Contents

7. Conclusion: influencing the policy process 141

Figures

Tables

Boxes

Acknowledgments

We are grateful to many colleagues including Andrea Migone of the Institute of Public Administration of Canada and Ben Cashore of Yale University for detailed comments received on the first edition, as well as the very helpful insights provided by reviewers commissioned by Routledge Press. Many at the Lee Kuan Yew School of Public Policy at the National University of Singapore also supported this project, especially Kishore Mahbubani, Kanti Bajpai, Eduardo Araral, and Kenneth Tan. We have used portions of the manuscript in Masters courses and executive education sessions at the school, and the response we received from students and trainees also helped us tremendously in improving the text. Our sincere thanks to all of you.

1 Introduction

Managing the policy process

Why is managing the policy process important?

With recurring environmental and financial crises, terrorism, continuing widespread poverty and inequality, and deepening concerns about climate change, the need for sound public policies has never been greater. Contemporary economic, social, and technological changes make the need for good policy and governance yet more vital. Addressing problems related to these issues and others necessitate governments to rise to the challenge of devising more effective policies.

These kinds of problems are too vast for communities and corporations, much less individuals, to resolve on their own: only governments have the potential to address such collective issues, especially when they work constructively with other governments and nongovernmental actors to do so. Organizing and managing the policy processes involved at national, subnational and international levels is a critical task and an important harbinger of successful policy-making and effective policy outcomes.

Understanding policy processes and policy-making activities and the behavior of key actors is thus essential for policy actors aspiring to influence policy development in a positive direction. This book seeks to provide key policy actors in government and in nongovernmental positions with lessons found in the many works in the policy sciences that deal with these issues and questions.

Empirical research, for example, shows that government policy and governance institutions are the strongest determinants of development, both economic and social (Lin and Chang 2009; Haggard and Kaufman 2016; Rodrik, Subramanian and Trebbi 2004). Conversely, weak institutions and the bad policies they often produce are commonly the largest determinants of development failures. Thus, in the mid-1950s, income, education, and health indicators for Myanmar (formerly known as Burma) and South Korea, for example, were broadly similarly, but within only a decade all these indicators were much higher in South Korea, largely due to the policy institutions and practices found in that country which allowed effective policies to be developed, enacted, and implemented. Success bred further success in Korea while interlocking policy, governance, and development failures in Myanmar deepened over several decades (Holliday 2012). As these two countries show, the rewards for enacting sound policies through effective management of the policy process are as high as the costs of getting them wrong; and the long-term performance differentials generated by policy choices made today can be staggering.

The surest way to ensure effective policies are made and implemented is to build institutions and processes for making and implementing them that avoid common errors and replicate the conditions and practices needed for success. How this can best be accomplished is what this book is about. The book is for all stakeholders involved in the policy process. It is built upon the premise that policy actors can overcome existing barriers that undermine their potential for contributing to policy success. To do this requires that they better understand the requisites and institutional supports for effective policy-making, and identify and seize opportunities to leverage their positioning within often crowded policy-making processes to influence outcomes.

A difficult policy world: the challenges of governance

Governments face many challenges in contemporary policy-making (see Van der Wal 2017). One growing concern is the increasing "wickedness" or complexities of policy problems. Uncertainties have always plagued policy-making. But the ability to predict how policy x will affect problem y and associated issue z over time has been increasingly seen as strained to the breaking point by:

- the ever widening interconnectedness of problems;
- the expanding range of actors and interests involved in policy-making; and
- a relentless acceleration in the pace of change and decision-making (Churchman 1967, Levin et al. 2012).

Another factor which makes policy-making increasingly difficult is the fragmentation in many countries of the societal, political, and policy institutions traditionally charged with organizing collective action in government. The polarization and fragmentation of public aspirations, ever rising expectations of government, and secular declines in public confidence and trust in government institutions also compound the challenges facing policy-

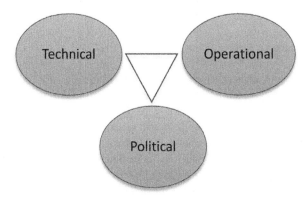

Figure 1.1 Policy challenges

makers. Together these institutional, political, and policy realities create what has been termed "super-wicked" problems, which pose three types of challenges to policy actors inside and outside government:

- **political** challenges linked to the need to gain agreement from key actors and the public on policy direction and content;
- **technical** or analytical challenges related to determining the most effective course of action; and
- **operational** challenges linked to effectively developing and implementing policy choices (see Figure 1.1).

Each of these three challenges is discussed in detail below and in the chapters which follow.

Political challenges

Policy-making is a quintessentially political process in that it affects who gets what, making it vital for policy actors to understand the political implications of their actions (Lasswell 1958). Merely understanding policy-making as an analytical exercise—identifying the costs and benefits of different policy alternatives, for example—is not enough; policymakers need also to come to grips with the political dynamics underlying the policy activities in which they engage. Successful policy actors need to survey the policy-making fields in which they themselves are situated, and in doing so:

- identify other actors involved in and affected by policies and policy-making;

- map out their essential interests, ideologies and relationships; and
- assess the waxing or waning of their sources of power and leverage within the process.

Policy-making is embedded in a world of formal and informal political compromises and deal-making. Policy actors need therefore to understand how and why to compromise—to acknowledge the trade-offs between policy theory and practice that may be needed to secure agreement among contending actors and interests on a particular course of action that government or other strong policy actors may desire. Indeed, policy actors may need to help craft such compromises, or to manage their consequences.

Consider (as we do throughout this book) the possible causes of policy failure. Ineffectiveness might on the surface stem from the poor design of an individual policy, or from incompetent or weak administration of the same. But often the real cause lurks elsewhere—in the failure to recognize and manage the contending interests of other policy actors. Examples are legion across levels and agencies of government itself, and may be magnified when government works cooperatively with the private or civil society sectors to formulate and implement policy.

Disagreements *between different levels of government*, if left un- or poorly managed, can also lead to contradictory policies that are mutually destructive of the aims of all. In federal countries, for instance, one level of government may promote coal extraction to produce electric power while another level tries to reduce greenhouse gas emissions (Scharpf 1994), a situation which requires management if either aim is to be achieved.

Within a single level of government, the goal of any given policy can be thoroughly clouded or undermined by the desires and strategies of different government agencies, each quite "rationally" pursuing incompatible or contradictory agendas. This is commonly the case, for example, where one ministry wishes to pursue an ambitious expansion policy in health or social welfare spending while fiscal gatekeeper organizations such as finance ministries or treasury boards wish to curtail budget deficits or government spending. Or agriculture ministries may continue to promote agricultural production at the expense of decreased water availability for industry and households, which may themselves be the subjects of major expenditure initiatives by ministries of public works and infrastructure expected to increase the latter (de Moor 1997). Again, such conflicts need to be anticipated and managed if either aim is to be accomplished.

It is also often the case that policies are formulated by governments and political parties in order to secure the support of politically powerful groups of economic or social actors at the expense of long-term public interests that may be underrepresented in the political system (Bachrach and Baratz

1970). In many countries, small groups of agricultural and business elites, for example, often exercise a virtual veto over reforms aimed at redistributing land or improving wages and working conditions for the large majority of the population (Patashnik 2008). But even where such conditions do not exist, political actors may try to appease clients in society and earn their support rather than act in the interests of the public at large.

Consideration of the political context in which policy-making occurs also helps us to understand why some policies are adopted despite having virtually no chance of having an impact on the ground at all. So-called "ideological" or symbolic policies are often used by political elites to cement their legitimacy among key supporters. With multiple ambiguous, non-prioritized, and largely non-measurable goals, such policies have little chance of being effective in achieving any but political constituency-building aims.

Technical challenges

In addition to the very significant political challenges, governments also face a variety of technical and analytical challenges in understanding policy problems and their root causes, and in devising solutions for them based on realistic estimates of future effects and outcomes (Pollock et al. 1993). There is often not enough information available on the historical or even current situation encountered by a government for it to fully specify the nature and scope of the policy problem itself, let alone its solution. Nor are the analytical tools that would help analyze available information, isolate cause and effect relationships, and inform effective policy action always available (Howlett 2015; Hsu 2015). In many countries and contexts, the available information and analytical tools are often manifestly inadequate in dealing with the growing complexity of problems (Parrado 2014). And the difficulties in acquiring and analyzing information are compounded by not knowing what to do with the findings.

Take the obesity problem in many countries as a good example. We know what causes it (high caloric intake and insufficient physical activity to burn it) and what the population needs to address the problem (fewer calories and more activity). What we do not know is what can be done to discourage the population from consuming more calories than they can burn (May 2013). Another example of a problem with high behavioral (and other kinds of) uncertainty is global warming and the adaptations necessitated by the ensuing changes in our climate. An even more immediate problem is terrorism; it has so many different origins and manifestations that it is impossible to devise solutions that would stymie all potential individuals and groups from turning to terrorist activities (May et al. 2009).

Such uncertainties need to be managed and, if possible, overcome. But policy-making in many countries is not helped by the generalist character of civil services found in them. Inherited from earlier times when problems were less pressing and complex, or when general expertise was adequate for most issues governments faced, public servants in many countries are still not generally expected, much less required, to be subject experts. This is notwithstanding the classic conception of the public service as being composed of "specialists" assisting "generalist" political masters. The reality is that most civil servants lack even basic training in the substantive areas in which they work (Howlett and Wellstead 2011; Howlett 2009) and often lack the skills and analytical competences needed to plug the information gaps and related uncertainties that plague decision-making and policy formulation and implementation. The health care sector, which attracts nearly one-tenth of global GDP, for example, is largely managed by public servants who lack both training and extended experience in the sector. Similarly, pension systems—another big budget item for most governments—are typically run by managers who lack basic training in actuarial estimates or in the politics of pension reforms (Stiller 2010). Policymakers need to address these technical capacity gaps if policies are to be effective.

Operational challenges

In addition to these political and analytical hurdles, policymaking also involves serious operational challenges. Organizing collective actions inevitably involves numerous individuals and agencies in complex deliberative and analytical processes. The making and implementing of effective policies require, at a minimum:

- well-defined administrative processes delineating the roles and responsibilities of different offices and agencies;
- adequate resources available for policies to be carried out;
- compliance and accountability mechanisms in place to ensure that all concerned are performing the tasks expected of them (McGarvey 2001); and
- the establishment of incentives that enforce not only minimum compliance on the part of agencies and officials with prescribed duties but also encourage them to seek improvements in their performance, something all too rare in many governmental organizations (Osborne and Gaebler 1992).

But making, implementing, and evaluating public policy is, of course, a collective effort. It is not sufficient for individual agencies and officials to function effectively. Governments need to ensure that officials and agencies work in unison towards shared goals. Coordinating and integrating the myriad efforts of large and diverse public agencies—across levels of government, and often in concert with actors in the private and non-profit sectors—is an extraordinarily difficult task (Vince 2015; Briassoulis 2005). Given that making and implementing policies almost always involves more than a few agencies, coordination is often hampered by such factors as:

- a "silo mentality," whereby each agency focuses on its own core responsibility while ignoring the objectives of other agencies with whom they must cooperate to achieve an overall policy objective;
- different organizational cultures and standard operating procedures, which make it difficult for actors in a network to share information and resources, and to coordinate operational details; and
- the existence of multiple-veto points in many implementation chains, whereby an actor can stop or dramatically slow down joint efforts.

The interconnectedness of policy problems increasingly requires agencies established in earlier eras to coordinate their efforts in order to achieve policy objectives. The single-minded outlook, culture, or operational tool-kit of any single agency can pose a major hurdle to the design and enactment of effective public policy (May 2014).

Policy functions and processes: design and management of effective policies

The ability to recognize, diagnose, and adequately address the interrelated political, organizational, and analytical complexities described above marks the litmus test for effective policy actors and public managers, and for the systems in which they work. Understanding the conditions and circumstances that promote policy effectiveness, and what it might take to institutionalize them, is the main focus of this book.

As described above, all governments face different levels and combinations of political, operational, and technical barriers which determine the enormity of their tasks and how and to what extent they may be overcome. While individual leadership (and luck) may produce good policy in the face of these challenges, the only way to ensure that good polices are consistently produced is to have the right institutions and processes in place (Tiernan 2015a; 2015b). Modern problems are too complex to be dealt with by individual leaders, no matter how capable they may be. And so being a capable leader in this context means employing one's leadership skills to *build appropriate policy institutions and processes*, in addition to handling the contingencies associated with any given policy problem.

In short, the main limitation on government ability to address policy challenges is the set of deficiencies in the processes by which policies are made, implemented, and evaluated. Governments need to design an effective process to identify emerging problems, generate and assess alternative solutions to addressing the root causes of the problems, implement them in ways that take the behavior of all stakeholders into account, and finally evaluate the performance of the policies in a way that allows correct lessons to be drawn about smart practices (Howlett Ramesh and Perl 2009). Designing policy functions and processes in a way that is simple enough to be operationally workable while being responsive to the demands of policy coordination and complexity is the difficult but unavoidable task of modern governance. Even where policy actors must take such processes and organizational parameters as given (i.e. not amenable to redesign or improvement in the short term), they must find ways to effectively manage within their limitations.

Understanding the policy process

The policy process consists of the performance of five vital activities: agenda-setting, formulation, decision-making, implementation, and evaluation. These policy activities can be thought of as unfolding in "stages" with some progression of policy-making from one stage to another (see Figure 1.2). Exactly in what order these activities occur and how they are linked together varies from case to case. Each is a discrete, albeit often interrelated, set of activities that often occurs in fits and starts in cycles of attention and inattention to certain issues by government (Downs 1972; Kingdon 1984; Teisman 2000).

Agenda-setting is about how perceived problems become policy problems that governments commit themselves to addressing (Kingdon 1984; Baumgartner and Jones 1993). Each society has hundreds, even thousands, of issues that citizens find to be matters of concern and which some would have the government do something about. Only a small proportion are actually taken up for consideration by policymakers. While there is a tendency to view agenda-setting as something confined to policymakers in the executive and legislative branches of government this is not entirely accurate; a variety of other actors such as the media, think tanks, nongovernmental organizations, and political parties also play a vital role (Kingdon 1984). Public managers at all levels in governments and civil society groups, however, are in a unique position to identify emerging policy issues through the programs with which they are involved. Public managers also often serve as a screening mechanism or as "gatekeepers" able to substantiate and verify and support (or not) various claims for attention among policymakers and the public at large. Most importantly, public managers can contribute to identifying and resolving significant policy issues that require sustained

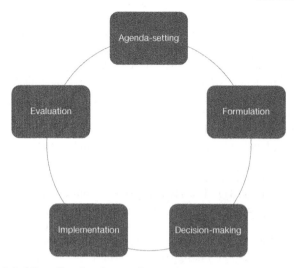

Figure 1.2 Public policy functions and processes

attention through their long tenures and experiences in office (Hicklin and Godwin 2009).

Policy formulation involves the development of alternative courses of government activity designed to address problems which may be on, or expected to appear on, the government agenda (de Leon 1992). Due to competition for their attention and/or the urgency of the issues they face, policymakers typically have only brief windows of opportunity to come up with actionable solutions, and such pressure can lead to erroneous choices from a short- or long-run perspective (Birkland 1998). Policy actors can help to foster the development of policy ideas long before these issues reach the policy agenda; in so doing, they may help improve both the chance of their issue being taken up and the likelihood of future policy effectiveness (Halligan 1995; Craft and Howlett 2012). They can also help to ensure that recognition of unresolved design issues, or of implementation challenges, is followed up in later stages of the policy-making process, since the attention of both the policymakers and the public to a particular issue may dwindle as new issues emerge (Downs 1972; Jones 1994).

Decision-making occurs throughout the policy process. In the sense used here, it involves governmental authorities deciding on a particular course of action which is expected to address some policy problem (March 1994). Such choices are absolutely critical, of course, in determining what action a government will take and how it will be implemented and, as such, are an indispensable part of policy-making and ultimately of policy success or failure. Often only senior echelons of the government are involved in this kind of decision-making, though they typically consult others in the government or civil society before arriving at decisions. This provides many opportunities for actors—lobbyists, interest groups, policy managers, and others—to influence the content and direction of the policy decisions (Clemens and Cook 1999).

Implementation is another key activity in the policy process. In it, policy is actually given form and effect (Hill and Hupe 2009). The critical influence that implementing officials at all levels in public service and within in civil society will have in determining policy success and failure on the ground rarely captures the public's or even policymakers' attention (Sabatier and Mazmanian 1981). The recurring and omnipresent inconsistencies between policy design and implementation found in many policy areas and jurisdictions suggest much improvement can be made through creative and discerning efforts by public managers and civil society groups to improve implementation and policy design (Goggin et al. 1990). And policies decided in the political arena are often broad and vague, leaving crucial details to public officials to work out (Epstein and O'Halloran 1994). This often provides a great deal of discretion to public servants—discretion that can sometimes serve to enhance policy implementation but that also raises create opportunities for localized corruption or other departures from policy intent (Scott 1969). In order to improve implementation, governments need to not only fully understand their options and spell out their decisions clearly, but also to provide incentives to implementers to improve implementation activities and disincentives towards administrative malfeasance, arbitrariness, and capriciousness (Deschenaux 2015).

Policy evaluation is a final critical policy activity. It involves the assessment of the extent to which a public policy is achieving its stated objectives and, if it is not, what can be done to improve it (Stufflebeam 2001). Evaluations must not only be clear about what lessons can be learned from past experience, but also ensure that they are designed in such a way that appropriate lessons are learned. Evaluations are often carried out by think tanks, interest groups, and other nongovernmental actors, but the direct access to information on policy performance enjoyed by public managers provides them with distinct advantages in this activity. However, such potential has often remained largely untapped. In part, due to many public managers' fears of being undermined by negative evaluations of their own work, this tendency to downplay evaluation can also arise from a lack of sufficient technical expertise within the bureaucracy to conduct complex program evaluations. Given that evaluation is an indispensable part of policy learning and policy-making, such barriers to its production and utilization need to be overcome (Etheredge 1981).

Actors in the policy process: policy "communities"

A typical policy actor may be heavily involved in some of these five policy activities, somewhat more involved in others, and not at all in others. But who are these actors and how do they interact?

To date, we have only talked about policy actors in general terms while occasionally mentioning such groups or organizations as civil society actors, governments, citizens, public servants, policy managers, think tanks, and others. In recent years, it has been broadly accepted that policies are not just made by agencies formally responsible for the issue but collectively by key stakeholders, both private and public (Hayward 1991). It is very common, for example, for scores, if not hundreds and perhaps even thousands, of people to be involved across many different kinds of institutions and organizations—from think tanks to legislatures and cabinet offices—in making and implementing a single policy. Think of the huge range of actors involved in the development of the Affordable Care Act ("Obamacare") in the US, finally enacted in 2010 after a multi-decade-long development process. Not only were state, local, and federal governments and legislatures, health care providers, pharmaceutical manufacturers, think tanks, and political parties heavily involved, but also the courts and the public through various forms of protest and electoral contests.

Because of their many attributes and activities, instead of discussing their individual role, analysts commonly refer to the role played by "communities" or "networks" of actors in policy-making. Building on earlier notions of "sub-systems," the conception proposes that policies are made by sets of sector-specific government and nongovernment actors who form a "policy community" or "issue network" (Heclo 1978). As Miller and Demir (2007) put it, policies are made not just by those in formal authority but by those "most affected, most interested, most expert, or most sentimentally attached to the issue." Policy communities comprise sub-sets of the governmental, nongovernmental, and international actors depicted in Figure 1.3 involved in specific policy issues or "sectors," such as health, the economy, automobiles, or telecommunications activities, among many others.

Governmental actors

The permanent players in the policy process, however, are governmental actors operating at subnational, national, and increasingly international levels who actually develop, decide upon, and implement public policies. Government officials are the primary actors in the policy process, notwithstanding the expansion of efforts to privatize government functions and expand the role of civil society and market players in the design and delivery of public services. Public policies are "public," after all, and in the modern era the

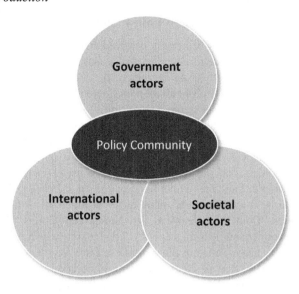

Figure 1.3 Actors in the policy process

state is the sovereign entity capable of speaking for and acting on behalf of the public. At least in the context of a reasonably democratic and capable state, its officials are the bearers of final authority, a fact that places them at the center of all policy processes. Legally, the authority to make and implement policies is the exclusive preserve of the government, though in democratic societies governments often choose to share this authority extensively with societal actors (Galanter et al. 1980), and for very weak governments (think of "failed" states, as an extreme case) *de facto* control over public sector resources may be highly diffuse by default.

Governmental actors include elected officials as well as appointed administrators. Elected officials include legislators and executive members, while appointees include civil servants and members of the judiciary. The exact role they play in policy-making depends upon the issue as well as the configuration of state institutions. The role of legislators in the policy process, for example, ranges from not very significant (in the case of some parliamentary systems in which the ruling party by definition controls the legislature and can "whip" or direct members to follow its lead), to substantial in presidential systems (where presidents and governors must negotiate constantly with individual members of congresses over passage of bills) (Olson and Mezey 1991).

It is true, theoretically and technically speaking, that for all governments —regardless of the nature of their political system—elected or appointed executive members are the "masters" of the policy process, while civil "servants" are tasked only to assist their masters in performing essential government functions. In reality, however, the longer tenure and experience of civil servants means they commonly play a much larger and deeper role in defining policy content than this theoretical view would suggest, even though final authority to make policy decisions would typically (though not always; think of certain central bank appointments or executive agencies) remain with the political executive. While ministers can and do launch major policy initiatives, the bureaucratic agency in charge of a policy sector normally plays a key role not only in implementation, but in all stages of the policy process (Overeem 2012).

The days are long gone, however, when policies were made by a single individual or even a single group within the government (Craft and Howlett 2012; Parson 2004). The great policy challenges of our time are too complex for either politicians or civil servants to be able to address on their own. Governments increasingly rely for expertise in dealing with problems upon groups and individuals outside the government, and need to find ways to work with them in policy-making. In past eras, this often involved finding ways to bring companies and other market actors into policy-making, often through activities such as contracting out government services or privatizing government firms. But greater participation and openness—often stemming from trends such as globalization and the rise of the internet and digital government—have also led to new modes of governance taking root along-side traditional market and state-based ones (Capano et al. 2015). These include a variety of new arrangements for the "co-production" or co-design and co-management of policies through formal and informal state and civil society interactions (Pestoff 2006; Pestoff et al. 2012). These activities—to take two examples, the use of parent-teacher associations to enhance and deliver educational services, or of disability associations to partner with government to serve the disabled—have raised both new challenges and new opportunities for governments, and have introduced a range of new actors— and growing complexity—into traditional policy processes.

Societal actors

The range of societal actors involved in the policy process and policy communities is potentially very large, since it is sometimes possible for individuals, acting as activists, litigants, or voters, to bring items to the government agenda. Such individuals may attempt to have an impact on policy through public and legal action, such as demonstrations or lawsuits, right up to and through the implementation and evaluation stages. (The efforts by individuals and advocacy groups to use the courts to overturn the nascent Trump administration's ban on travelers and refugees from seven predominantly Muslim countries is a case in point.) However, it is more common for policy communities to have a modest number of identifiable players, and to feature leaders and representatives from interest groups, religious organizations, companies, labor unions, associations, think tanks, or other kinds of policy research organizations interacting with each other over relatively long periods of time (McFarland 1987).

These actors command different kinds of resources, from economic power to knowledge, that stem from the nature of the organizations they lead or represent; and these resources, and the skill with which they wield them, determine the ability of each actor to influence government thinking and attention on various issues (Cawson 1978). Among interest groups, for example, businesses and business associations are generally the most powerful, with an unmatched ability to affect public policy through their direct control over investment and, hence, indirectly, over the jobs and economic prosperity that most governments desire. Labor too can occupy a powerful position among social groups in countries with high unionization rates, though it is typically less powerful than business, on whom organized labor also relies for job creation and wages (Harrison 1980; Panitch 1977).

Surprising as it may appear, "the public" often plays a rather small and only indirect role in the public policy process (Brooks 1985). This is not to say that its role is inconsequential, as it provides the backdrop of norms, attitudes, and values against which the policy process unfolds. However, in most liberal democracies, rather than the citizens themselves, it is their representatives who are entrusted with the task of governing. But insofar as these representatives depend on their appeal to voters to win elections, they need to take public opinion into account. And elections provide an opportunity for political parties to present their policy platforms, their appeals to the public for why they should be given control over legislative and executive offices. Once in existence, parties often work to put innovative strategies forward in order to win elections, including preparation of policy packages to appeal to voters. These packages are often a vital source of public policy agendas that public managers and other public servants must be prepared to address after the election (Von Beyme 1984).

Another significant set of societal actors in the policy process is made up of researchers working at universities, research institutes, and think tanks who develop "bespoke" or "off-the-shelf" packages of ideas and instruments politicians and policy community members can use in developing and defending policy proposals and decisions (Prince 1983). These organizations maintain an interest in a broad range of policy problems and use their expertise and positioning to enable them to develop and put forward a comprehensive perspective on the issues facing governments. Their research tends to be directed at proposing practical solutions for public problems or, in the case of some think tanks, finding evidence to support the ideologically driven positions they advocate on behalf of those who fund them. This sets them apart somewhat from academic researchers at universities and research organizations who tend to have broader interests and do not necessarily seek to find or advocate practical solutions for policy problems. Explicitly partisan research is also generally frowned upon in academia (Cohn 2007), although some have argued that it is on the increase.

In societies with a relatively free press or open internet, traditional and newer social media can play an important role in bringing issues onto the public and government agendas. Such media may publicize and criticize policy proposals as well as policy performance or non-performance (Spitzer 1993). The development of information and communication technologies has greatly enhanced the media's ability to shape public opinion on public problems (Criado et al. 2013) and their ability to name and blame a policy for a problem or a "solution" for failing to resolve it, which can sometimes force an issue onto or back onto a government agenda. The extensive reporting of the health implications of smoking, for example, heavily influenced the development of antismoking legislation passed in many countries over the past half century.

However, this does not mean that the media directly controls agenda-setting and other policy processes. Often, the media itself suffers from a lack of access to information, poor reporting, and a host of other factors that limit its ability to set government agendas or otherwise influence decision-making, implementation, or other policy activities (Patterson 1998). The media is also far from homogeneous. The proliferation of newer media actors, and the explosion of "news," both fake and real, consumed via social media platforms, including Facebook and websites dedicated to specific ideological viewpoints in recent years, have proven to be game-changers for the media's role in policy advocacy. They represent avenues for a range of actors to influence the policy process in new and sometimes surreptitious ways. They also have led to a dilution of advocacy power among mainstream outlets, and a decline in the general level of societal trust in all forms of public affairs reporting, a phenomenon sometimes called the advent of a "post-fact world" (Fukuyama 2017).

International actors

International actors constitute a third general category of policy community membership, but one which varies considerably by policy area (Reinicke 1999). These actors may be individuals working as advisors or consultants to national governments or donor organizations, or members of international organizations with the authority under international agreements to regulate their members' behavior. International actors are more likely to participate and act effectively in policy sectors in which there is an international agreement sanctioning their intervention (Keohane and Milner 1996). The central place occupied by the International Monetary Fund (IMF) in the international monetary regime, for example, enables its officers to interfere in the details of public policy-making in many nations facing serious financial or fiscal problems. An even more significant resource is the possession of theoretical and practical expertise in a policy sector. Many international organizations—the World Bank and World Health Organization (WHO), for example—are repositories of immense expertise in policy issues. As a result, national governments often rely upon them when making policies, giving them significant influence in domestic policy processes (Mahon and McBride 2008). The financial resources that international organizations can dispense to governments form another source of influence that can help move specific items, or specific approaches to certain problems, onto government agendas.

The nature and role of policy communities

Policy communities exhibit a number of discernible features (Van Waarden 1992; Atkinson and Coleman 1992). First, as mentioned above, these policy communities are centered on a functional sector, such as banking, energy, education, or health care. Members are expected to represent their organizations rather than their own perceptions and interests (though this is not always the case, or even possible). Second, the relationships among public and private actors within a functional sector forming a community are typically more informal than formal; rarely are the roles and responsibilities of the communities or their members specified in an official document or their existence even officially acknowledged. Third, the relationships between members are often horizontal, rather than hierarchical, in the sense that members relate to each other as equals rather than as subordinates or superordinates. Fourth, members are bound by shared core values: while conflicts among members are common, they typically center on policy details rather than core goals and functions. Fifth, and relatedly, the relationships in a community are durable and extend across issues and over time; they do not disband after an issue has been addressed. Sixth, each member of a policy community has resources—financial, informational, electoral, etc.—that are of value to others, and this forms the basis for exchange and cooperation among them (Rhodes and Marsh 1992).

The size and specific membership of policy community varies considerably by sector. In the banking sector, for example, the policy community is likely to consist not only of central banks and the ministry of finance, but also managers of large banks and perhaps other financial institutions, as well as established think tanks and academics in the field.

The policy community in the agriculture sector, similarly, would comprise the agriculture and perhaps environment ministries plus a range of different farmer advocacy groups, major agro-industrial and agricultural biotechnology firms, and researchers specializing in farming issues. The effectiveness of a policy community depends on its membership's comprehensiveness and coherence, among other things.

Originally developed to describe how policies were actually made, the concept of *policy capacity* is used increasingly in a normative sense; that is, proponents use the concept to not only describe how policies are made and implemented in their view, but also how they *should* be made. Proponents argue that governance by close-knit groups (or policy communities) can be efficient and effective; it ensures policies are made by those with knowledge in the area and who have an interest in its success, unlike more traditional conceptions of a public service run by faceless and neutral bureaucrats.

But policy-making by policy communities (where they exist) suffers from limitations that cannot be ignored. First, policy communities exclude citizens and are therefore undemocratic. Second, the line separating a (beneficial) policy community from (much less so) crony networks is fuzzy and may be breached easily, leading to grave consequences in terms of policy effectiveness and the realization of the public or common good. Most importantly, in the contemporary era the sector-centeredness of policy communities militates against solutions to problems, such as poverty and climate change, that increasingly cut across sectors (Jochim and May 2010).

The exact range of societal and the specific state actors involved in the policy process depends to a great extent on the nature and characteristics of the policy issue, overall political system, and the policy sector in question. It is also a function of the policy activity concerned (May 1991). Agenda-setting, for example, is often an "open" activity in which a variety of actors drawn from within and beyond the government are involved. While governments sometimes play the lead role in highlighting a problem and defining its scope and depth, they are often reactive: responding to demands made by civil society groups and the media.

Policy formulation, by comparison, often sees the involvement of fewer nongovernmental actors as bureaucratic players assume a central role in canvassing, fleshing out, and assessing policy options. Though they may consult civil society actors for greater clarity and legitimacy, bureaucratic actors often work in relative secrecy (from the public's perspective) (Halligan 1995). Decision-making outside of elections and referenda is always the narrowest and most closed policy function, typically performed exclusively by relatively small numbers of political executives in cabinets or administrative agencies. Indeed, official secrecy often prohibits the public from even knowing how and on what basis decisions were made. Conversely, the number of actors in policy implementation may range from only a few—confined to a lead line agency in the case of traditional civil service delivery, for instance—to a much larger spectrum of governmental and nongovernmental actors in the case of "co-production," in which representatives from various sectors collaborate in a reciprocal relationship in the production of knowledge or public services (Brandsen and Pestoff 2006). Modern governance is to a large extent characterized by increasing efforts to expand the implementation process to include nongovernmental organizations and private firms (Torfing 2012).

Policy evaluation is also a large and "open" area despite often having been viewed as an activity conducted by inside experts on an episodic basis. Following the realization that such evaluations are often ineffective in improving outcomes, there are increasing efforts being made to open up the evaluation process to include a broader range of governmental and nongovernmental actors, including the public, through such devices as social media. In this way, the evaluation function within the policy process, and its contribution to "policy learning," might be take place on a more continual basis (Howlett Ramesh and Perl 2009), and in theory might help the process to benefit from a broader range of perspectives as well. On the other hand, many commentators have noted that the proliferation of participants in policy analysis and evaluation has done little to stem the politicization of findings and perspectives; all powerful sides in a policy arena can and do roll out studies and evaluations purporting to "objectively" prove their point of view (Daviter 2015).

Again, however, the exact range of actors involved in each activity depends heavily on the policy sector in question. Defense and, to a lesser extent, foreign affairs are usually conducted behind closed doors and involve far fewer actors than activities such as education or health that typically involve a much larger variety of governmental and nongovernmental actors, often at multiple levels of service delivery and policy activity (Hooghe and Marks 2003).

Managing the policy process: policy acumen, analytical skills, and managerial expertise

It follows from the above discussion that appropriate institutional arrangements and structured policy processes are imperative for making effective policies and implementing them effectively. The institutional arrangements should allow deliberation and the utilization of knowledge and expertise in policy-making (Nutley et al. 2007). The policy process, in turn, should be able to:

- recognize emerging problems and understand their sources;
- develop, analyze, and compare alternative solutions;
- select the most effective solutions;
- implement them effectively by creating the conducive conditions; and
- assess the performance of chosen solutions and revise or replace them as needed.

The success of a policy system rests on the degree to which it facilitates the ability of a government and society to move forward to meet the most important chronic and emergent challenges of its time. Yet chronic policy underperformance, spectacular policy failure, or "window dressing" activities that simply perpetuate the status quo are all too common to varying degrees in all governments.

What marks the difference between high- and low-performing policy systems is the key question this book addresses. Our answer centers on the way in which government institutions and management practices structure the relationships among governmental, societal, and international actors.

One key is to create effective relationships among policy actors by structuring policy communities in such a way that they are focused on problem-solving and the promotion of broader interests rather than (only) the pursuit of self-interest. Policy communities that are cohesive, yet transparent and open—especially to new actors and ideas—play a very significant role in determining whether policy problems may be handled in an effective way (see Figure 1.4). The challenge is to establish policy communities which perform these functions in an integrated manner (Vince 2015; Meijers et al. 2004).

In reality, however, it is rare to find policy-making systems that are equipped to address complex problems in an integrated, coherent, and adaptive fashion (Howlett and Ramesh 2014). Policy actors are often handicapped not only by narrowly defined self-interests with short-term time horizon, but also by the lack of appreciation of the complexities of the problems they encounter and the constraints and opportunities they face. Institutions and practices conducive to responding to such complexities at system level are often conspicuous by their absence. In such circumstances, policy actors' ability to integrate and simultaneously address political, operational, and technical challenges determines the overall effectiveness of their policy actions while the five key policy functions provide them ample opportunities for intervention. This book focuses on identifying key points of potential

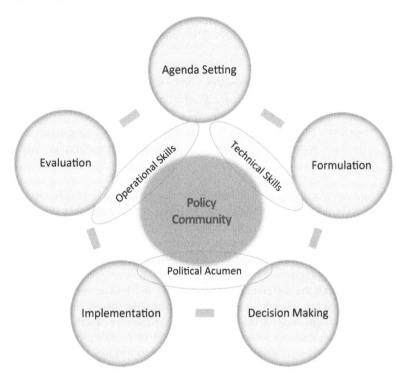

Figure 1.4 The policy system: actors, skills, and policy process

influence on the policy process. We argue that policy actors can make a crucial contribution in their respective domains by leveraging their *political acumen, analytical skills,* and *managerial expertise,* subjects that serve as a major focus and theme of this volume.

Policy or political acumen. Policy acumen consists of the accumulated knowledge of, and experience in, the policy process. It starts with an understanding of the key players, their key interests, and their strategies and resources. It also rests on a broad understanding of policy practices in other countries and/or different policy sectors. This knowledge and experience forms a solid basis for judgment about policy feasibility: what will work in one's specific circumstances and contexts, and what will not. Contrary to expectation, policy actors are often particularly weak in the development of policy acumen, due to their lack of training in public policy and related fields, their limited exposure and access to key stakeholders in policy system (Pal and Clark 2016), and the inherent complexity of (often emergent) policy problems.

Analytical skills. The second capacity necessary for effectively participating in the policy process is analytical skills for diagnosing a situation or problem and for developing appropriate strategies to address it. For example, analytical tools such as political mapping and stakeholder analysis enable policy actors to assess the support for existing and proposed policy measures, while cost-benefit analysis and other policy analysis techniques help them to compare the consequences and costs of various options available. While not all policy actors may be directly involved in conducting formal analysis (instead depending on their colleagues or policy network partners), it is critical for them to be familiar with the potential and limitations of the various analytical tools, in order to be intelligent and critical consumers of analyses produced by others (Howlett 2015).

Managerial expertise. Policy actors' capacities to perform key managerial functions—such as planning, organizing, staffing, budgeting, coordinating, and monitoring—also significantly shapes their ability to participate effectively in the policy process. For example, managerial expertise may allow them to exert greater influence in agenda-setting, where their efforts in sustaining attention onto key public issues are particularly critical. In addition, their managerial expertise may provide opportunities to lead the development of alternative forms of network management, or to better coordinate and direct the activities of a multitude of actors involved in the policy process (O'Toole and Meier 2010).

In this book, we discuss these capacities and policy challenges and reflect on how they can be met in an integrated manner. The chapters in this book show how many policy actors need to change the way they define their goals, conceptualize and select alternative means of reaching the goals, implement their choices, and evaluate their performance so that corrections may be made to existing policies and superior outcomes attained. The book demonstrates not only the complexity and challenge inherent in the attempt to manage the policy process, but also the potential opportunities for doing so that might be unlocked by well-prepared, high-capacity policy actors.

References

Atkinson, M. and Coleman, W. (1992). "Policy Networks, Policy Communities and the Problems of Governance." *Governance*, 5(2), 154–80.

Bachrach, P. and Baratz,M. S. (1970). *Power and Poverty: Theory and Practice.* New York: Oxford University Press.

Beyme, K. von. (1984). "Do Parties Matter? The Impact of Parties on the Key Decisions in the Political System." *Government and Opposition*, 19(1), 5–29.

Birkland, T. A. (1998). "Focusing Events, Mobilization, and Agenda Setting." *Journal of Public Policy*, 18(1), 53–74.

Brandsen, T. and Pestoff, V. (2006). "Co-production, the Third Sector and the Delivery of Public Services: An Introduction." *Public Management Review*, 8(4), 493–501.

Brooks, J. E. (1985). "Democratic Frustration in the Anglo-American Polities: A Quantification of Inconsistency Between Mass Public Opinion and Public Policy." *Western Political Quarterly*, 38(2), 250–61.

Briassoulis, H. (Ed.) (2005). *Policy Integration for Complex Environmental Problems: The Example of Mediterranean Desertification*. Aldershot, UK: Ashgate.

Capano, G., Howlett, M., and Ramesh, M. (Eds.) (2015). *Varieties of Governance*. Studies in the Political Economy of Public Policy. Houndmills, Basingstoke, Hampshire; New York: Palgrave Macmillan.

Cawson, A. (1978). "Pluralism, Corporatism and the Role of the State." *Government and Opposition*, 13(2), 178–98.

Clemens, E. S. and Cook, J. M. (1999). "Politics and Institutionalism: Explaining Durability and Change." *Annual Review of Sociology*, 25, 441–66.

Cohn, D. (2007). "Academics and Public Policy: Informing Policy-Analysis and Policy-Making," in Dobuzinskis, L., Howlett, M., and Laycock, D. (Eds.), *Policy Analysis in Canada*. Toronto: University of Toronto Press, pp. 574–98.

Craft, J. and Howlett, M. (2012). "Policy Formulation, Governance Shifts and Policy Influence: Location and Content in Policy Advisory Systems." *Journal of Public Policy*, 32(2), 79–98. doi:10.1017/S0143814X12000049.

Criado, J. I., Sandoval-Almazan, R., and Gil-Garcia, J. R. (2013). "Government Innovation through Social Media." *Government Information Quarterly*, 30(4), 319–30. doi:10.1016/j.giq.2013.10.003.

Daviter, F. (2015). "The Political Use of Knowledge in the Policy Process." *Policy Sciences*, 48(4), 491–505.

De Moor, A. P. G. (1997). *Perverse Incentives: Hundreds of Billions of Dollars in Subsidies Now Harm the Economy, the Environment, Equity and Trade*. San Jose: Earth Council.

Deschenaux, J. (2015). "Lessons for Employers from a Massachusetts Marijuana Lawsuit." *HRMagazine*, 60(9), 27–30.

Epstein, D. and O'Halloran, S. (1994). "Administrative Procedures, Information, and Agency Discretion." *American Journal of Political Science*, 38(3), 697–722. doi:10.2307/2111603.

Fukuyama, F. (2017). "The emergence of a post-fact world", www.project-syndicate.org/onpoint/the-emergence-of-a-post-fact-world-by-francis-fukuyama-2017–01 [accessed March 31, 2017].

Galanter, M., Blankenburg, E., Klausa, E., and Rottleuthner, H. (1980). "Legality and Its Discontents: A Preliminary Assessment of Current Theories of Legalization and Delegalization," in *Alternative Rechtsforen Und Alternativen Zum Recht*. Bonn: Westdeutscher Verlag, pp. 11–26.

Goggin, M. L., Bowman, A. O. M., Lester, J. P., and O'Toole, L. J. (1990). *Implementation Theory and Practice: Toward A Third Generation*. Glenview: Scott, Foresman/Little, Brown.

Haggard, S. and Kaufman, R. R. (2016). *Dictators and Democrats: Masses, Elites, and Regime Change*. Princeton: Princeton University Press.

Halligan, J. (1995). "Policy Advice and the Public Sector," in Peters, B. G. and Savoie, D. T. (Eds.), *Governance in a Changing Environment*. Montreal: McGill-Queen's University Press, pp. 138–72.

Harrison, R. J. (1980). "Natural Resources and the Constitution: Some Recent Developments and Their Implications for the Future Regulation of the Resource Industries." *Alberta Law Review*, 18(1), 1–25.

Hayward, J., Rustow, D. A., and Erickson, K. P. (1991). "The Policy Community Approach to Industrial Policy," in *Comparative Political Dynamics: Global Research Perspectives*, 381–407. New York: HarperCollins.

Heclo, H. "Issue Networks and the Executive Establishment," in King, A. (Ed.), *The New American Political System*. Washington D.C.: American Enterprise Institute for Public Policy Research, pp. 87–124.

Hicklin, A. and Godwin, E. (2009). "Agents of Change: The Role of Policy Managers in Public Policy." *Policy Studies Journal*, 37(1), 13–20.

Hill, M. and Hupe, P. L. (2009). *Implementing Public Policy: An Introduction to the Study of Operational Governance*. 2nd ed. Thousand Oaks, CA: Sage Publications Ltd.

Holliday, I. (2012). *Burma Redux: Global Justice and the Quest for Political Reform in Myanmar*. New York: Columbia University Press.

Hooghe, L. and Marks, G. (2003). "Unraveling the Central State, but How? Types of Multi-Level Governance." *American Political Science Review*, 97(2), 233–43.

Howlett, M. (September 2015). "Policy Analytical Capacity: The Supply and Demand for Policy Analysis in Government." *Policy and Society*, Special Issue on The Dynamics of Policy Capacity, 34(3), 173–82. doi:10.1016/j.polsoc.2015.09.002.

Hsu, A. (September 2015). "Measuring Policy Analytical Capacity for the Environment: A Case for Engaging New Actors." *Policy and Society*, Special Issue on the Dynamics of Policy Capacity, 34(3), 197–208. doi:10.1016/j.polsoc.2015.09.003.

Jochim, A. E. and May, P. J. (2010). "Beyond Subsystems: Policy Regimes and Governance." *Policy Studies Journal*, 38(2), 303–27. doi:10.1111/j.1541-0072.2010.00363.x.

Keohane, R. O. and Milner, H. V. (1996). "Internationalization and Domestic Politics: An Introduction," in *Internationalization and Domestic Politics*, 3–24. New York: Cambridge University Press.

Lasswell, H. (1958). *Politics: Who Gets What, When, How*. New York: Meridian.

Lin, J. and Chang, H. (September 2009). "Should Industrial Policy in Developing Countries Conform to Comparative Advantage or Defy It? A Debate Between Justin Lin and Ha-Joon Chang." *Development Policy Review*, 27(5), 483–502. doi:10.1111/j.1467-7679.2009.00456.x.

Mahon, R. and McBride, S. (2008) *The OECD and Transnational Governance*. Vancouver: UBC Press.

May, P. J. (1991). "Reconsidering Policy Design: Policies and Publics." *Journal of Public Policy*, 11(2), 187–206.

May, P. J., Sapotichne, J., and Workman, S. (2009). "Widespread Policy Disruption and Interest Mobilization." *Policy Studies Journal*, 37(4), 793–815.

May, C. (February 2013). "Agency and Implementation: Understanding the Embedding of Healthcare Innovations in Practice." *Social Science & Medicine*, 78, 26–33. doi:10.1016/j.socscimed.2012.11.021.

McGarvey, N. (April 2001). "Accountability in Public Administration: A Multi-Perspective Framework of Analysis." *Public Policy and Administration*, 16(2), 17–29. doi:10.1177/095207670101600202.

Meijers, E., Stead, D., and Geerlings, H. (2004). "Policy Integration: A Literature Review," in Meijers, E., Geerlings, H., and Stead, D. (Eds.), Policy Integration in Practice: The Integration of Land Use Planning, Transport and Environmental Policy-Making in Denmark, England and Germany. Delft: Delft University Press, pp. 9–24.

Miller, H. T. and Demir, T. (2007). "Policy Communities," in Fischer, F., Miller, G. J., and Sidney, M. J. (Eds.), *Handbook of Public Policy Analysis: Theory, Politics and Methods*. New York: CRC Press, pp. 137–47.

Olson, D. M. and Mezey, M. L. (1991). *Legislatures in the Policy Process: The Dilemmas of Economic Policy*. Cambridge, UK: Cambridge University Press.

Osborne, D. and Gaebler, E. (1992). *Reinventing Government*. Reading: Addison-Wesley.

O'Toole, L. J. and Meier, K. J. (2010). "In Defense of Bureaucracy—Public Managerial Capacity, Slack and the Dampening of Environmental Shocks." *Public Management Review*, 12(3), 341. doi:10.1080/14719030903286599.

Overeem, P. (2012). *The Politics-Administration Dichotomy: Toward a Constitutional Perspective, Second Edition*. CRC Press, 2012.

Panitch, L. (1977). *The Canadian State: Political Economy and Political Power*. Toronto: University of Toronto Press.

Parrado, S. (2014). "Analytical Capacity," in Lodge, M. and Wegrich, K. (Eds.), *The Problem-Solving Capacity of the Modern State: Governance Challenges and Administrative Capacities*. Oxford: Oxford University Press.

Patashnik, E. M. (2008). *Reforms at Risk: What Happens After Major Policy Changes are Enacted*. Princeton, NJ: Princeton University Press.

Patterson, T. E. (January 1998). "Time and News: The Media's Limitations as an Instrument of Democracy." *International Political Science Review*, 19(1), 55–67. doi:10.1177/019251298019001004.

Pollock, P. H., Lilie, S. A., and Vittes, M. E. (1993). "Hard Issues, Core Values and Vertical Constraint: The Case of Nuclear Power." *British Journal of Political Science*, 23(1), 29–50.

Prince, M. (1983). *Policy Advice and Organizational Survival*. Aldershot: Gower.

Reinicke, W. H. (1998). *Global Public Policy: Governing without Government?* First Edition. Washington, DC: Brookings Institution Press.

Rhodes, R. A. W. and Marsh, D. (1992). "New Directions in the Study of Policy Networks." *European Journal of Political Research*, 21, 181–205.

Rodrik, D., Subramanian, A., and Trebbi, F. (June 2004). "Institutions Rule: The Primacy of Institutions Over Geography and Integration in Economic Development." *Journal of Economic Growth*, 9(2), 131–65. doi:10.1023/B:JOEG.0000031425.72248.85.

Sabatier, P. A. and Mazmanian, D. A. (1981). *Effective Policy Implementation.* Lexington: Lexington Books.

Scharpf, F. W. (1994). "Community and Autonomy: Multilevel Policy-Making in the European Union." *Journal of European Public Policy*, 1, 219–42.

Scott, J. C. (December 1969). "Corruption, Machine Politics, and Political Change." *American Political Science Review*, 63(4), 1142–58. doi:10.1017/S0003055400 263247.

Spitzer, R. J. (1993). *Media and Public Policy.* Westport, CT: Praeger.

Stiller, S. (2010). *Ideational Leadership in German Welfare State Reform: How Politicians and Policy Ideas Transform Resilient Institutions.* Netherlands: Amsterdam University Press.

Tiernan, A. (March 2015a). "Craft and Capacity in the Public Service." *Australian Journal of Public Administration*, 74(1), 53–62. doi:10.1111/1467-8500.12134.

Tiernan, A. (September 2015b). "The Dilemmas of Organisational Capacity." *Policy and Society*, Special Issue on The Dynamics of Policy Capacity, 34(3), 209–17. doi:10.1016/j.polsoc.2015.09.004.

Torfing, J. (2012). "Governance networks", in Levi-Faur, D. (Ed.), *The Oxford Handbook of Governance.* Oxford: Oxford University Press.

Van der Wal, Z. (2017). *The 21st Century Public Manager.* UK: Palgrave. Chapter 2 and 3.

Vince, J. (June 2015). "Integrated Policy Approaches and Policy Failure: The Case of Australia's Oceans Policy." *Policy Sciences*, 48(2), 159–80. doi:10.1007/s11077-015-9215-z.

Waarden, F. van. (1992). "Dimensions and Types of Policy Networks." *European Journal of Political Research*, 21(1/2), 29–52.

2 Agenda-setting

Agenda-setting is a label for the process by which governments decide which issues need their attention and prioritize amongst them. It involves, among other things:

- the determination and definition of what constitutes the "problems" that subsequent policy actions are intended to resolve;
- preliminary exploration of the possible solutions to such issues;
- assessment of the extent and nature of political support for any kind of action to resolve them (Dery 2000, Kingdon 1984, Mukherjee and Howlett 2014).

In the abstract, a successful agenda-setting process is thus one that is able to prioritize and assess the root causes of problems, and to focus the lion's share of attention onto those problems with a reasonable chance of resolution within a reasonable time period, utilizing a reasonable amount of government resources. However, this is often not the case. Rather governments typically have a great deal of trouble understanding the sources of problems, estimating what is feasible and what is not, and controlling the sequencing of issues to be dealt with (Skodvin et al. 2010). In many cases, they are unable to exercise control over the issues that appear on their agendas; issues may be driven instead by factors such as natural calamities, partisan political maneuvering, and fickle public concerns driven by media headlines (Levin et al. 2012). Dealing with these process- and substance-related problems is essential both to agenda management and to understanding why policy actors act the way they do.

The difficulties governments face in agenda-setting begin with the very definition of a what is a policy "problem" needing action. As Kingdon (1984) noted, a "problem" is not the same as a "condition," which is some aspect of social life that may not be amenable to correction by government (even though it may be a source of public or government concern). A good example of a "condition" is human aging, broadly considered to be inevitable and outside the bounds of government control. While aspects of aging—such as elderly poverty or elderly care—may involve related issues that can be amenable to policy intervention and thus become "policy problems," "aging" in itself is a condition of life that governments cannot alter, not a "problem" *per se*. A problem, then, is the undesirable effect of a condition that is amenable to government action (Peters 2005). Hence the fact that airplanes crash, for example, is a condition linked to gravity which makes some accidents inevitable. But air traffic safety and aircraft maintenance are problems that can be addressed through, for example, the development of air traffic control systems and standards or, in the case of aircraft mainten-ance, regular inspections and maintenance standards and protocols (Rochefort and Cobb 1994).

Having said that, problems vary in their "tractability"—the degree of difficulty involved in developing and implementing solutions to them, whether due to cost or other factors (Hisschemoller and Hoppe 1995). A problem such as deaths due to car collisions might be effectively and affordably mitigated by, for example:

• mandating seat belt installation and use;
• traffic law enforcement;
• reduction in poor driving behaviors such as speeding and drunk-driving; and
• improving car safety during the manufacturing process by introducing "crumple zones" and air bags in cars.

In contrast, problems such as homelessness may be less tractable, as they might involve a staggering array of issues, such as:

• family life and living patterns;
• job preparation and employment trends;
• the education system;
• the nature of housing and real estate markets and landlord-tenant rela-tionships;
• drug, alcohol, and sexual abuse;
• issues linked to disabilities and the effectiveness of the health and mental health systems, etc.

Some problems deeply rooted in human behavior such as cigarette smoking and drug and sexual abuse, for example, are especially pernicious and difficult to root out or correct, making them highly "intractable" (Cnossen 2005).

Notwithstanding newspaper columnists, pundits, and media commentators who typically present the causes and nature of policy problems and the solutions to them as simple and self-evident, and hence the fault of venal, unintelligent, or ideologically blinkered politicians and civil servants for their failure to be corrected (Rose and Parsons 2015), in reality the opposite is often true. Problems with tractable characteristics—sometimes referred to as "well-structured" or "tame" problems (Simon 1973)—are quite rare in the real world of public policy, not least due to the fact that easily tractable issues are "low-hanging fruit" which typically have already been the subject of earlier policy interventions and in many cases greatly mitigated (at least as compared with initially very high levels).

To return to our car accident example, implementation of the more feasible and cost-effective among the measures noted above may have a significant *initial* impact on fatalities (reducing the fatality rate from a to b), leading to a sense in which *further* reductions (reducing further from b to c) prove to be relatively more difficult; the problem might have stabilized and become less amenable to intervention—more "intractable"—at any given level of effort. Recent years have seen an *increase* in traffic deaths due to distracted driving (e.g. use of mobile phones while driving), with few policy interventions as yet demonstrated to be effective. A similar dynamic may exist with efforts to reduce infant mortality rates. While large gains are initially achievable through targeted and relatively low cost, high-impact interventions like child immunization, further gains would depend on more complex and long-term efforts to strength health systems.

In some cases, problems are so successfully addressed that they arise much less frequently on government agendas—only when, for example, a very high-profile airline crash focuses attention onto some previously unexpected or unresolved aspect of an issue such as air traffic control. This was the case, for example, in 2014–2015 when two Malaysia Airlines aircraft crashed in unexpected ways; one disappearing without trace from radar screens on an otherwise regular flight, and the other being shot down over a warzone when governments in the region failed to close down commercial air traffic in an area filled with surface-to-air missiles and warring aircrafts.

These examples show that even for problems deemed to be relatively tractable, policy efforts take place in a complex, dynamic environment. This is even more true in the case of the much more common example of policies attempting to address much less tractable issues, such as the ill-structured or "wicked" problems discussed in Chapter 1. These problems have:

- boundaries subject to dispute;
- causes that may be unknown or poorly understood; and
- potential solutions that are highly uncertain and/or subject to deep disagreement among technical experts and social and political actors (Rittel and Webber 1973; Churchman 1967).

Such problems are occurring more frequently on government agendas as citizens, NGOs, and government agencies search for or demand ameliorative action on a wider range of problems linked to boundary-crossing conditions such as global warming.

Highly intractable issues can appear and disappear from policy agendas in a pattern that Anthony Downs (1972) called an "issue-attention" cycle. In it, immediate concerns and calls for action run up against the difficulties and costs involved in correcting or altering relevant policy behavior. Government and public attention drifts elsewhere until the issue is again raised to the forefront of public or government attention by some event and/or interest group. The problem of gun violence in the United States (including suicides, accidents, homicides, and periodic mass shooting events) provides one of the best examples of this process in recent years. Efforts common in many countries to limit or control access to weaponry which have proved effective in preventing such massacres are stymied by constitutional and interest group impediments in the US. Corrective action becomes extraordinarily difficult due both to extremely high rates of gun ownership and proliferation (a condition that may render many policies attempted in other settings technically ineffective if adopted in isolation) and to interest group dynamics. As a result, even mass public outrage following repeated mass shooting incidents (such as the Newtown massacre of 20 children and six adults from a single gunman with using a semi-automatic weapon) has, to date, failed to secure adoption of even modest gun control measures (Erbing et al. 1980).

Governments face other challenges in agenda-setting beyond issues of agenda control and the tractability of issues. Consider two. First, the poor framing of public problems often leads to government and public preoccupation with ineffective and wasteful solutions—preoccupation that may crowd out attention to more feasible solutions. Certainly, many social media and media commentators and pundits (but also politicians more interested in constituency building than problem-solving) contribute to this dysfunction.

Second, many critical public problems fail to reach official policy agendas, while relatively minor concerns—or concerns affecting narrow interest groups—do. A prominent cause for this is the nature of the interest articulation and aggregation systems present in a country or jurisdiction; these can favor the concerns of minor groups of "special" interests over more general "public" ones. The attention paid by many governments to tax breaks for the richest and wealthiest group of citizens and businesses—those capable of hiring lobbyists and public relations firms to press their claims for exemptions and special treatment—is far greater than that paid to issues such as gender inequality or child poverty. This is the case despite the fact that the latter issues affect many more people in much more serious ways than a lower capital gains exemption. But issues such as poverty and inequality are also much less amenable to clear solutions or to sustained and focused public pressure, given their diffuse character and the voluntary nature of groups and individuals concerned. Mounting a sustained lobbying and public education effort becomes much more difficult for such groups than for tax lawyers and their clients.

NGOs and other nongovernmental actors can and do take these processes and potential outcomes into account as they attempt to make their voices heard in policy-making circles. Governments and public managers are well-positioned to facilitate or hinder such efforts; they can, for example, ease the process of agenda-access for broadly constituted public interest groups, while making the same more difficult for narrow or private ones or vice versa (Cobb and Ross 1997; Rochefort and Cobb 1994). While public agencies are well-positioned to tackle these and other defects in agenda-setting and thus improve policy processes and outcomes, this potential remains largely untapped. This is not least due to the widespread perception that public managers' responsibility is confined to administrative and organizational tasks—the implementation of a given mandate handed down from above, a long-standing normative viewpoint often termed the politics-administration dichotomy (Rosenbloom, 2008)—rather than to the political and technical considerations that characterize agenda-setting.

In this chapter, we describe the nature of agenda-setting processes in more detail. We also explore various opportunities, circumstances and strategies that policy actors can employ to play a meaningful role in agenda-setting and to make agenda-setting both more facilitative of effective policy outcomes and more democratic.

The basics of agenda-setting

What is agenda-setting?

Agenda-setting is sometimes defined as the process by which the demands of various groups in the population are translated into items that governments consider for action. This definition is closely linked with the idea that public policy-making is driven primarily by the actions of nongovernmental actors—to which government would react (Cobb et al. 1976). Empirical evidence, however, has shown that in most countries concerns about certain policy problems are raised more often by members of governments rather than (or in addition to) social groups. In addition, it is sometimes the case that proposed solutions to problems precede the articulation of problems, such that agenda-setting becomes less about problem definition *per se* than about how actors attempt to attach their preferred policies to recognizable "problems" (Kingdon 1984, Beland and Howlett 2016). The adage "to a hammer everything looks like a nail" is one way of expressing this paradoxical quality in agenda-setting.

Regardless of how it actually arises, however, the policy agenda is a list of issues or problems to which governmental officials and others in the policy community are paying some serious attention at any given time. Agenda-setting is thus, as set out above, about a government recognizing that a problem is a "public" problem worthy of its attention and not simply an issue affecting only a few a people, or a background "condition" about which it can do very little and that must rather be endured (Rochefort and Cobb 1993; Dery 2000).

Agenda-setting is concerned with the initial processes of issue identification and policy initiation, and with the manner in which these processes affect subsequent policy-making activities undertaken by governments. It is a process that is:

- nonlinear in the sense that so-called solutions (proposed policies, programs, technologies or interventions) can be advanced before any stable problem definition is achieved, and items may appear on agendas in a cyclical or some other form;
- political as well as technical, in the sense that perceptions of the magnitude and scale of problems, and of the feasibility of potential solutions, are often equally (or more) important than actual evidence of the same; and
- located within a complex network of state and societal organizations, policy subsystems and actors, including experts and various members of epistemic communities, political coalitions and instrument constituencies or groups of actors promoting particular policy solutions (Baumgartner and Jones 1991; 1993).

Both governmental and nongovernmental actors involved in any aspect of policy-making must be fully aware of these realities. They must also be aware of consequences of these realities, both for agenda-setting itself and for later stages or tasks involved in policy-making as discussed in subsequent chapters.

What is the content of agendas?

Given the different configurations of conditions, institutions, and actors found in different jurisdictions, it is not surprising that the actual content of policy agendas differs across governments and time periods. That is to say, agenda items differ greatly between countries and jurisdictions in terms of the substance or content of agenda issues and the timing of their entrance into the process (Dowding et al. 2015).

In general, agenda formation depends on the nature of the economic and social circumstances in which people live and governments operate. In China, for example, the government's top agenda items in the late twentieth century focused on spurring economic growth and addressing chronic problems in social service delivery. In the first decade of the twenty-first century China's policy agenda shifted on the economic front away from production and supply concerns towards more consumption- and safety-oriented concerns, including threats to food safety and growing air pollution. In France and Japan, on the other hand, priorities in the later period included the reform of the pension system for public sector employees, and on health and immigration concerns—with both issues spurred largely by shifting demographics and the aging of their population (Pritchard 1992). These are phenomena that China too will face, but at a later date given the structure of its population demographics. As noted above for problem tractability, agenda formation needs to be placed in the context of changing social, economic, and political conditions, and of the adoption and effects of previous rounds of policy adoption.

As discussed in Chapter 1, policy communities—actors involved in defining and interpreting a problem and identifying solutions to it—play a significant role in bridging the formal government agenda and the informal public one. The "image" a policy problem has within a policy community—how it is named, claimed, blamed, and framed by different policy actors—heavily influences a problem's articulation, deliberation, and resolution (Baumgartner and Jones 1993). Hence, when a problem such as unemployment is portrayed as a technical and economic issue rather than a social one, economic experts in the policy community may dominate policy-making, and solutions can be discussed within a frame of immigration targets, apprenticeship quotas, or tax burdens. When the ethical, social, or political aspects of the problem assume the center stage, however, a much broader range of policy community participants might be involved. For example, as if the problem of unemployment is framed as being the result of unequal and unjust distributions of income, wealth, or opportunities, then actors such as political parties, trade unions, religious organizations, and social justice activists may rise in salience. (The causal relationship may be reversed: the question of which issue frame dominates agenda-setting will flow in large measure from the relative strength of the different contending policy actors involved.)

Policy actors need to understand these aspects of agenda-setting if they are to respond appropriately to the social and political concerns raised by their constituents and clients. They must understand, for example, the material interests of both social and government actors in relation to any particular issue, the institutional and ideological contexts in which they operate, and the potential for change in the circumstances that shape debates on public issues.

Furthermore, the nature of the issue at hand may influence the ability of any actor to affect the timing and entrance of a problem onto a societal or government agenda. Some issues—for example, adjusting resource allocation across industrial or social welfare portfolios—afford policy actors greater opportunity and discretion for deciding on the time and circumstance of their entrance onto a policy-making agenda; in other cases events or problems—such as those critical threshold or time-delimited consequences—force an agenda item onto the front burner of government attention and compel action, regardless of whether a government or any policy actors want to consider it at all, or at that specific point in time (Birkland 1998; Levin et al. 2012). Consider examples such as these:

- the 9–11 attacks on the World Trade Center in New York, and many other terrorist attacks in Europe and elsewhere;
- rising sea levels for various Pacific island nations, which in some cases have forced leaders to consider large-scale relocation of their population;
- the Syrian refugee crisis that saw European leaders scrambling to respond to contradictory demands from all sides.

These examples concern momentous, even catastrophic events of great magnitude. The great majority of issues afford more discretion and leeway to the gatekeepers of government agendas, as they decide if and when to deal with other subjects. The construction of a new highway or hospital, for instance, may well be left for consideration until immediately prior to an election, or some other circumstance thought to favor government interests.

Phases in agenda-setting

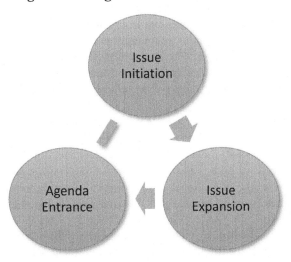

Figure 2.1 Agenda-setting phases

Issue initiation

Initial demands for government action can come from inside and/or outside governments, described as inside initiation and outside initiation respectively (Cobb et al. 1976). In the case of inside initiation, the government controls many aspects of problem definition, framing, and issue articulation. In such cases, officials can often place an issue onto the formal agenda of the government even in the absence of any public pressure, or even any publicly recognized grievance. There may be considerable debate within a government over the issue, but the public may well be unaware of the policy and its development until its formal announcement; in some cases, such as with certain highly technical issues or security-related policies, no formal announcement of the policy adoption or change may be forthcoming at all. A good example of inside initiation is pension policy. Pension reforms are often tied to demographic changes that alter actuarial projections of fund profit or loss. They thus reflect fiscal pressures as opposed to popular clamor to work longer (admittedly an unlikely proposition) or to increase contributions.

Inside initiation also includes situations in which influential groups with special access to the government initiate a policy without the general public's involvement (Fischer 2003). The wish to exclude public scrutiny may reflect special characteristics of the sector involved—such as with national security issues—but may also stem from political considerations (for example, government fear that an issue might be hijacked or stalled by opponents).

For example, certain critics have alleged that international lending agencies often initiate unpopular policy reforms in this manner; many aspects of banking and financial regulation as well as trade negotiations—areas in which narrow but well-mobilized and well-resourced actors have much to gain or lose—have also been linked to such agenda dynamics.

Both of these cases are quite different from the case of *outside initiation*, in which issues appear on the government agenda as a result of "pressure" from individuals, groups, and organizations outside government (Jones 1994). This is often thought by many members of the public to be the only way in which issues can, or should, arise in policy-making, though as shown above this is clearly not the case. In this better-known pattern, issues arise first within a societal space first; and then—if nongovernmental actors play their cards well, circumstances are propitious—issues expand sufficiently in the public realm so as to find space within the government's informal, and eventually its formal, policy-making agenda.

How common such a pattern varies by country and jurisdiction. Some systems of government are more open to outside agenda-setting than others (Cobb et al. 1976). The state of California—and Switzerland—both witness frequent citizens' initiatives that are put to vote by the entire electorate due to constitutional provisions for referenda. Other countries, such as Belarus, Brunei, and Turkmenistan, and perhaps to a lesser extent China and Kazakhstan, discourage or informally suppress the formation of interest groups not controlled by the government; in others, such as North Korea and Saudi Arabia, such groups are generally illegal. In yet other cases, such as Singapore and Nicaragua, state actors may, due to constitutional design, capacity, or tradition, so dominate the public sphere that outside initiation remains a relatively rare phenomenon.

Issue articulation

There are multiple ways to frame a particular policy issue in a given context, and the ways in which problems are defined and (re)framed dictates how they are treated in subsequent policy activities (Felstiner et al. 1980). For example, if the problem of the low school enrolment rate for girls in many countries is defined merely as an education problem, it might not receive adequate attention in a country where gender inequality is the cultural norm. But if it is framed as a developmental problem affecting a population's health, housing, labor productivity, economic growth, and poverty levels, it may receive a rather different reaction and a higher priority, motivating swifter public investment in female education.

Both state and non-state actors attempt to construct "policy monopolies" that control the definition and image of a problem. That is, policy actors and managers encourage the framing of problems in ways that expand the constituency in support of their issue prioritization and, ultimately, resolution (Cobb and Edler 1972). Government-sponsored activities such as education and information campaigns, for example, can affect the kinds of issues perceived by the public as problems and how they are framed in the public imagination.

A sudden crisis which foists a problem onto the public agenda can help to break down an existing image "monopoly," allowing different views of policy problems and solutions to compete in public and government discourses. This loss of agenda control by state actors can also happen when government communication efforts are weak, fragmented, and/or generally unconvincing, allowing other state and societal actors to rally support for their own naming and framing of issues. This was the case, for example, in 2006 when the issue of US involvement in war in the Middle East was predominantly framed within the US media not as "how to achieve victory" and "whether" to withdraw troops (frames that the government of the day would have preferred), but as "how to cut losses," and "why" troops were still deployed at all.

Issue expansion

Regardless of how popular a policy initiative may be, or how strong its internal champions are, its induction onto the formal agenda of government can be problematic. Outside actors encounter more difficulty in seizing control of the agenda than do their internal government counterparts, and must be backed by expensive and time-consuming public issue and education campaigns, in addition to special interest lobbying, for their issues to make it onto the agenda independently (Dion 1973; Hansford 2004). The mobilization of support can occur through a range of activities, from organizing letter-writing or media campaigns to picketing and civil disobedience. Good examples of such processes in many countries include campaigns:

- against drunk-driving, led by groups such as Mothers Against Drunk Driving (MADD);
- for the legalization of certain drugs such as marijuana; and
- for gay, lesbian and transgender rights.

In all of these cases, groups have engaged in sustained and sometimes successful public education and lobbying efforts. While inside actors may be able to skip the "social mobilization" phase as they seek to push their issue onto the government's informal agenda, their task is not easy; in order to move their agenda onto the formal agenda, they must still compete in a crowded agenda field with other issues being promoted inside governments (by other inside initiators) and by outsider initiators who are meeting with success in their own efforts.

Of course, the formal agenda of government and the informal public agenda are not independent of each other. Government activities (such as government-sponsored public education and information campaigns), as well as more direct measures (such as the funding of specific public works projects), have an effect on the kinds of issues defined by the public as "problems," providing a kind of "feedback loop" between government action and public problem perception and definition (Fischer 2003; Hammond 1986). This highlights the complex relationships between the formal agenda of the government and the informal public agenda, which must be understood by all public actors, both governmental and nongovernmental, if they hope to have their policy issue, and their particular framing of it, advance towards policy adoption, and ultimately to achieve their policy goals.

Of course, not every issue promoted for attention by inside or outside initiators is seriously advanced for policy adoption or impact. For example, actors in any political arena may attempt to use issue framing as a means to position themselves favorably among their supporters, or to deflect attention from defeats in other areas. Such phenomena—which underscore that "[b]ecause politics is driven by how people interpret information, much political activity is an effort to control interpretations" (Stone 2002)—are a reminder that the process of agenda-setting, like much else in the policy-making process, is not as "rational" and technical as it is sometimes made out to be.

Agenda entrance

Timing is critical in agenda-setting. The concept of a "policy window" or "opportunity opening" through which an issue may be placed onto a government agenda drives home the point that the agenda-setting process is sometimes governed by contingencies that force problems to the forefront (Kingdon 1984). We see this, for example, when an airliner crashes and forces changes to safety practices; or when an election produces an unexpected turnover in key decision-makers and brings a new set of policy issues associated with the winner onto the policy agenda. The year 2016 saw several such vicissitudes—witness the multidimensional shockwaves emanating from the British electorate's decision to exit the European Union, and Donald Trump's victory in the 2016 US presidential election.

Four types of policy windows are common. Policy actors need to be aware of these different types of opportunities for agenda entrance, and be prepared to take advantage of them when they occur. These include:

- *routinized windows*: in which routinized procedural events such as budget cycles dictate agenda openings;
- *discretionary windows*: where individual political preference on the part of decision-makers dictates window openings;
- *random windows*: where unforeseen events, such as disasters or scandals, open agenda windows; and
- *spill-over windows*: where related issues are drawn into already opened windows in other sectors or issue areas, such as when railway safety issues arise due to the increased attention paid to airline or automobile safety due to some crisis or accident (Howlett 1998).

In order to use window openings, policy actors need the capacity to identify and act upon the kinds of windows likely to be present in their areas of interest. The high-profile nature of random windows might lead to the impression that agenda-setting is uncontrollable, but most policy windows open quite predictably. Legislation comes up for renewal on schedule, for instance, creating opportunities to change, expand, or abolish certain programs; policy actors neglect such predictable action points at their own peril.

Regardless of their source, however, open windows are scarce and often short-lived; actors must be prepared for them in advance. Opportunities come, but they also pass. Windows do not stay open long and if a chance is missed, another must be awaited, sometimes for a very long time. The strategies of agenda control that policy actors employ, then, should include the ability to prepare for the different kinds of windows that may open, a subject that requires the analytical capacity to predict events and take advantage of them.

Challenges in agenda-setting

Agenda-setting is perhaps the most critical stage in the policy process, since without it there would be no policy to speak of. It is also commonly the least well understood by neophyte policy actors and inexperienced managers. The process by which policy problems vying for the attention of policymakers are sorted out and defined is highly complex with multiple hurdles that those charged with dealing with emerging problems must consider. It is critical to understand that not all public problems are acknowledged as problems by governments. Indeed, only a few are ever even formally considered by governments for resolution (Peters 2005; Dery 2000). This means there is a good chance that a problem prioritized on the public agenda will fail to make it to the government's agenda; it is highly unlikely to do so without some assistance from active, well-informed, and well-positioned policy actors.

Problem analysis is a notable challenge at this stage, for several reasons. First, the separation of symptoms from the cause of a problem can be notoriously difficult. When people talk about policy problems, they are often talking about the symptoms of problems. Even officials specializing in a sector often confuse the two and define the agenda in ways that set the policy process on a wrong course. Understanding the causes of problems requires sufficient information, skills, and time to analyze—all of which may be in short supply for policy actors ranging from interest groups to government agencies. It is also more convenient to focus on symptoms rather than causes; causes are quite simply more contentious. Almost everyone agrees that widespread poverty and increasing income inequality are policy problems. Speak of causes, though, there are deep divisions on all sides, with different actors pushing for acceptance of, and action based upon, their own preferred frames and evidence. Governments, for their part, are often unable to critically assess the contending interpretations, and often either give in to the most powerful pressures or let their own prejudices define how the problem causes are framed (Schneider and Ingrams 1997).

Second, the policy agenda is often dominated by demands for responses to crises, and due to the pressures for action and short timescales associated with them, governments are often forced to take some easily available course of action—one that may ameliorate the symptoms of the problems, but that is unlikely to address their root causes (Birkland 2004). Policy actors also prepare for and manage the contingencies and uncertainties that face them—problems that may occur, rather than those in front of them. This is the standard challenge of disaster management activities around the globe; but the analytical and organizational resources that it requires should not be underestimated—and simply may not exist (or be made available) within the system (Howlett 2016).

A closely related phenomenon is that until a crisis breaks out, a public problem may struggle to be placed onto policy agendas. However, often the costs of dealing with a crisis are much higher than would be the case if pre-emptive measures had been taken to prevent its occurrence. A good example of this is the failure of many developing countries to deal with HIV/AIDS through preventive programs until the disease was already widespread.

Third, agenda-setting is sometimes used by politicians as a means to pay lip service to policy problems in order to score political points rather than to make efforts to actually address problems (Fischer 2004; Saward 1992). Countless examples of such "window dressing" can be found in both developed and developing countries. This is the case in many countries, for example, with the phenomenon of homelessness or spousal abuse, which many politicians claim is a major concern while continuing to put in place symbolic statements rather than developing realistic plans or processes to deal with them.

Fourth, governments often tend to define problems in ways that absolve them of the responsibility for causing or aggravating a problem, and/or whose resolution involves the least effort on their part. While such blame avoidance may benefit the government, it misdirects policy efforts and in most cases will eventually lead to the problem remaining unresolved—or even worsening. "Blaming the victim"—blaming rape victims in the criminal justice context, or obese individuals in health policy context, for example—allows governments to avoid responsibility for improving security or nutrition standards (Stone 1989).

Fifth, the "overcrowding" of the policy agenda is a pervasive problem in agenda-setting. At its root lies the reluctance of many politicians to say "no" to the inclusion of specific group problems on government agendas because of pressure from their constituencies and special interest groups. The result is a saturation of the policy agenda, when there are neither the resources nor the time to deal with so many problems effectively. Such saturation diffuses the limited resources that might have been used to deal with a smaller agenda more effectively (Birch 1984).

Finally, agenda-setting may be hijacked by the media and/or special interest groups with little concern for overall government or other social priorities, or for the connections of specific problems to others. For example, in many countries business interests have in recent decades been particularly adept at defining social policy problems as issues requiring market-oriented solutions. This has in some cases affected how basic services such as water and transportation are delivered to the population through firms or public-private partnerships, regardless of how these services might be best delivered in particular circumstances.

Regardless of how it occurs, the poor understanding or framing of public problems often leads to the persistence of ineffective and/or wasteful "solutions" to them. And, if governments prioritize the wrong policy issues, the chances of developing sound policies may be missed from the very beginning, despite the efforts that might be made in subsequent stages of the policy process.

Strategies for policy actors in agenda-setting

Many policy actors are well placed to deal with the challenges mentioned above. This is especially true of public managers. Where they enjoy professional status as career public servants, for example, they can have substantial impacts in directing, intensifying, or *sustaining* attention onto particular policy issues over an extended period of time. Second, due to their expertise and experience, public managers may be well-positioned to identify and predict changing social needs in the policy environment. They may also serve as a *reality check* (or fact verifiers) both for policy ideas coming from the top and bottom, thus helping to "screen" and assess issues raised by politicians and social actors in terms of their cost and feasibility. Third, their control over access to information with regard to the outcomes of existing policies and programs provides public managers with a unique channel to shape the policy priorities of other actors such as interest groups and research institutes. Finally, public managers, as prominent actors in the policy process, can ensure that various channels for policy issues to reach policy agendas, both internal and external to government, coexist and complement each other (Hammond 1986).

On the other hand, public managers also face obstacles that impede their role in agenda-setting. First, they may lack perceived legitimacy in agenda-setting if their role is defined too narrowly—if they are seen, for instance, as only the *implementers* of policy. Second, they may have little room to maneuver if there is tight control over their budgets, information, and activities. Third, most public managers lack the communication, persuasion, and negotiation skills essential for effective engagement with politicians and the public in agenda-setting. Fourth, they may occupy a marginal position within a policy community and experience difficulty working across organizational or sectoral boundaries to confront complex problems. Finally, they and their agencies may lack the analytical capacity—skills, resources, and necessary information—required for the accurate diagnosis of policy problems (Peters 2016).

Other actors in the private or civil society sector face similar capacity issues. Most do not have the kinds of resources required to create and sustain public interest in their issues and problem frames over the length of time required to have them noticed by governments (Hansford 2004).

In the case of both public sector managers and other policy actors, several strategies are available to try to overcome these limits.

Leveraging to shape problem definition

There are many ways to define (frame) a policy problem; and, of course, how a problem is defined will shape what is done about it (Stone 1989). Policy actors can employ their experience and expertise to map the policy environment, assess the implications of different interpretations, and channel their efforts toward ensuring that more productive and feasible interpretations prevail. The causes of a problem as expressed by the public, the media, or politicians may be very different from their actual root causes; policy actors can use data and theoretical frameworks (such as the analysis of market failures or government failures) to guide the search for a sound, empirically valid, or "evidence-based" problem definition (Skodvin et al. 2010). Some actors, including many government agencies and larger NGOs like Greenpeace, are able to play a major role in issue naming, blaming, claiming, and framing (Felstiner et al. 1980)—either informally through their contacts with societal actors, or formally through their influence over the media, think tanks, or academics. In this way, they can influence the direction of policy-making at the agenda-setting stage by naming and framing an issue in such a way as to promote, authenticate, or legitimize the "claims and blames" of specific sets of policy actors.

Governments usually try to control the formal policy agenda. However, the fact that this agenda is inextricably linked to the larger social agenda of perceived problems means that it is easy for a government to lose control over its own agenda and to find itself reacting to a seemingly random set of concerns and issues raised by the population and by contingencies that may arise. This must be avoided, because careful sequencing of issues and solutions is required if effective policy-making is to take place. In many instances of *outside* initiation, for example, policy actors within government may be frustrated by the definitions and frames attached to an issue by external actors. This is not to say that policy actors within government cannot influence the definition of a problem or the types of proposed solutions, only that they may not be able to control the timing of an issue's emergence. Outside initiators, in contrast, have their work cut out for them. They must have the requisite political resources and skills to outmaneuver their opponents in both issue framing and in manufacturing (or taking advantage of) opportunities to propel the issue onto the government's agenda.

In *inside* initiation, policy actors inside the government enjoy more leeway in defining and redefining policy problems, and in searching for solutions, than is the case for *outside* initiation. Inside actors are typically also better able to control the timing of an issue's emergence as well as the ways in which it proceeds into official policy-making procedures. This greatly aids their ability to integrate various demands and concerns into bundles of integrated policies.

In some cases, for example, there may be considerable debate within government over an issue such as climate change mitigation, but the public may well be kept in the dark about the policy and its development until its formal announcement. The policy may be specified in some detail, or it may include only general principles whose specification will be worked out later. While some public managers may feel that a secretive process would avoid lengthy delays in the policy formulation stage, there are risks and drawbacks to this approach: greater transparency early on can help raise the likelihood of a favorable public reaction to a new policy, support that could be crucial in the decision-making and implementation stages. The need for transparency and wide consultation is heightened where policy success requires attitudinal changes of the public or institutional reforms that affect multiple organizations. In such cases, public managers and government leaders alike would do well to consider a strategic public relations campaign aimed at mobilizing public support for their decisions. Reform of the pension system for public sector employees in France or alteration to the subsidies paid to Greek or Polish farmers, for example, are examples of reforms that may be initiated from within the government, but that cannot move forward without adequate mobilization efforts.

In the case of society-driven initiation, social actors need to be able to access information relevant to their cause. Public managers may find themselves in a position to help or hinder initiators' articulation of issues and concerns; for example, they might provide information on substantive issues or governmental processes that might help outside policy initiators navigate complex routes onto the official government agenda. Alternatively, public managers might help secure such access by organizing or institutionalizing stakeholder consultations and other forms of participatory policy-making (Cobb and Ross 1997). The existence of "freedom of information"-type provisions governing the public sector may affect the types of information available to the public; but even where enabling legislation exists, the capacity of the public interest groups to anticipate their informational needs and navigate their way through official requests can be quite limited.

Public managers can also work to involve both those actors that are already intimately involved in policy proposals ("insiders") and those likely to become involved at some point in the future ("outsiders") through various kinds of consultative activity. In addition, policy actors outside government can try to attain representation on key consultative bodies established by law or custom (Saward 1992). Such consultative processes typically include both short- and long-term mechanisms to provide recommendations to the government concerning policy problems. Advisory committees, commissions, task forces, and roundtables are all forms of government-appointed bodies tasked with developing problem definitions acceptable to both social and state actors. Where such consultation is meaningful, networks of policy actors may emerge with a greater capacity to successfully negotiate specific proposals through the remaining stages of the policy process. The appointment of members of the public to these and other institutional bodies in itself can be a means of increasing the representation of unorganized public interests, both at the agenda-setting stage and throughout the entire policy process (Dion 1973), though the effect in practice will depend on the merits of the selection process and the effectiveness with which specific bodies influence policy-making.

Managing agenda entrance strategically

Policy actors both inside and outside governments need to be able to identify and manage the different types of windows that lead to agenda entrance. "Routinized" windows are the most common opportunity to raise a substantive policy issue. Every political and administrative system has its own annual cycles and rhythms marked by key milestones, for example "Speeches from the Throne" in Canada or Britain, the "State of the Union" address in the U.S. context, or annual legislative tabling of budget estimates in many countries. These act as opportunities for the consideration of new policy initiatives and the (re)evaluation of ongoing ones (Howlett 1998). Astute actors must make themselves aware of these cycles and related internal deadlines, and plan ahead to ensure that attention to the problems they are working on is heightened through these opportunities.

Most "discretionary" windows are also not random, and can be managed (if not always predicted or controlled) by policy actors (Birkland 2004). Seemingly "random" matters sometimes reach the agenda as a result of a pressing problem or "focusing event"—think of a corruption scandal or public health crisis. But to take advantage of such opportunities, different policy actors (government agencies, think tanks etc.) can and do prepare more or less "off-the-shelf" preferred policy solutions that essentially "wait" on opportune moments for their introduction (Craft and Howlett 2012). Crises, disasters, symbols, and other focusing events only rarely carry a subject to policy agenda prominence by themselves (Birkland 2004); they need to be accompanied by both political support and an available solution, and usually succeed only when they reinforce some pre-existing perception of a problem.

The extent to which institutional procedures allow, promote, or prevent the occurrence of entrepreneurial political activity by policy actors is a significant factor in determining the propensity for predictable and unpredictable windows to occur. Where the allocation of time to debate bills and make statements in legislative institutions, for example, remains largely in the hands of government—as in parliamentary systems—the opportunities for discretionary agenda-setting are highly restricted. Where time allocation is somewhat more flexible—as in countries with presidential political systems—the opportunities for individual policy initiatives is much greater. Public managers should be aware of these differences in political regimes, and their consequences for the timing of agenda initiatives, and plan their activities accordingly. Policy actors chronically overestimate their ability to create their own policy windows. Formal government agendas can be jammed to overflowing by extensive budgetary and housekeeping responsibilities, by revisions to established polices, and by pressing problems arising from various crises. During such periods governments are engaged mainly in reacting to the demands of outside political forces rather than shaping their own agendas. Policy actors can at times expend much time and effort in futile attempts to open policy windows that are simply untimely. Waiting for either an institutional window or a crisis window to open might be more advisable, but can itself be subject to considerable uncertainty.

Strategic alliances between state and non-state actors

Policy actors can also establish strategic alliances with non-state actors through regular consultations with key stakeholders to enhance their effectiveness in agenda-setting (Baumgartner and Leech 2001). Consultation exercises can provide an opportunity for stakeholders and interest groups to organize themselves so as to facilitate articulation and aggregation of public grievances. Such cooperation among different policy initiators outside the government is often required if an issue is to successfully proceed through to the governmental agenda and beyond. If this cooperation is not forthcoming, or if the goals of the government and societal groups are too diffuse, the government might be able to neutralize or co-opt certain groups in order to move forward what it believes to be an important agenda item (Saward 1992). This occurred in several prominent cases in the US recently in areas such as coal-mining regulations and pipeline approvals.

Policy actors also often try to "get out in front" of an issue and facilitate the convergence of views among different social groups, rather than simply waiting for the opposition to their proposals to coalesce and then attempt to overcome it. Encouraging public participation is a key method of state-led agenda-setting that can trigger the mobilization of public support, stimulate "outside initiation," or legitimize an "inside initiation" process. Such processes range from relatively passive public hearings and opinion polling (requiring only a response to a political survey) to the attendance of the representatives of political parties, interest groups, or other individuals at formal hearings.

In most market economies, industries and businesses also can have a strong impact on agenda-setting (McFarland 1987; Salisbury et al. 1987); as a result, governmental and social actors should pay close attention to powerful business groups and their diverse interests. These actors can directly engage with the media, and can use their prodigious resources (often pooled in industry-specific lobbying efforts) to directly fund campaigns, policy advocacy efforts (their naming, claiming, blaming and framing agenda-setting activities) and more passive policy monitoring. Such actors are also typically well-positioned and well-prepared to use policy openings to benefit their specific interests, often at the expense of more general or public interests.

Conclusion: the need to manage the agenda-setting process

Agenda-setting is where public policy-making starts. Unless a problem gets onto the official agenda, government will take no action on it. How a problem comes to be viewed as a problem, however, involves complex social and political processes as well as changing circumstances, such as the emergence of a crisis, and these complicate policy actors' roles in agenda-setting. To avoid being overwhelmed by these factors, policy actors need a sound knowledge base, strong analytical skills and resources, and a well-crafted but flexible strategy. This chapter has offered pointers in this direction.

The inclusion of a problem in the government's policy agenda is, however, only a start towards crafting some action that can be implemented to help resolve a problem. Governments must engage in two further sets of activities—policy formulation and decision-making—before it is able to take tangible action towards solving a problem. We now turn to policy formulation, the next activity in this process.

References

Baumgartner, F. R. and Jones, B. D. (1991). "Agenda Dynamics and Policy Subsystems." *Journal of Politics* 53(4): 1044–74.

Baumgartner, F. R. and Jones, B. D. (1993). *Agendas and Instability in American Politics*. Chicago, IL: University of Chicago Press.

Baumgartner, F. R. and Leech, B. L. (2001). "Interest Niches and Policy Bandwagons: Patterns of Interest Group Involvement in National Politics." *The Journal of Politics*, 63(4), 1191–213.

Beland, D. and Howlett, M. (2016). "Why Solutions Precede Problems." *Governance*, 29(3), 393–409.

Binderkrantz, A. (2005). "Interest Group Strategies: Navigating between Privileged Access and Strategies of Pressure." *Political Studies*, 53, 694–715.

Birch, A. H. (1984). "Overload, Ungovernability and Delegitimization: The Theories and the British Case." *British Journal of Political Science*, 14, 136–60.

Birkland, T. A. (1998). "Focusing Events, Mobilization, and Agenda-Setting." *Journal of Public Policy*, 18(1), 53–74.

Birkland, T. A. (2004). "'The World Changed Today': Agenda-Setting and Policy Change in the Wake of the September 11 Terrorist Attacks." *Review of Policy Research*, 21(2), 179–200.

Churchman, C. W. (1967). "Wicked Problems." *Management Science*, 14(4), B141–42—B141–42.

Cnossen, S. (2005). *Theory and Practice of Excise Taxation: Smoking, Drinking, Gambling, Polluting and Driving*. Oxford: Oxford University Press.

Cobb, R. W. and Elder, C. D. (1972). *Participation in American Politics: The Dynamics of Agenda-Building*. Boston, MA: Allyn & Bacon.

Cobb, R. W. and Ross, M. H. (Eds.) (1997). *Cultural Strategies of Agenda Denial: Avoidance, Attack and Redefinition*. Lawrence, KS: University Press of Kansas.

Cobb, R., Ross, J. K. and Ross, M. H. (1976). "Agenda Building as a Comparative Political Process." *American Political Science Review*, 70(1), 126–38.

Craft, J. and Howlett, M. (2012). "Policy Formulation, Governance Shifts and Policy Influence: Location and Content in Policy Advisory Systems." *Journal of Public Policy* 32(2), 79–98.

del Río, P. (2014). "On Evaluating Success in Complex Policy Mixes: The Case of Renewable Energy Support Schemes." *Policy Sciences*, 1–21. doi:10.1007/s11077-013-9189-7.

Dery, D. (2000). "Agenda-Setting and Problem Definition." *Policy Studies*, 21(1), 37–47.

Dion, L. (1973). "The Politics of Consultation." *Government and Opposition*, 8(3), 332–53.

Downs, A. (1972). "Up and Down with Ecology—The 'Issue-Attention Cycle'." *Public Interest*, 28, 38–50.

Dowding, K., Hindmoor, A., and Martin, A. (May 2015). "The Comparative Policy Agendas Project: Theory, Measurement and Findings." *Journal of Public Policy*, 36(1), 1–23.

Erbing, L., Goldenberg, E. N., and Miller, A. H. (1980). "Front Page News and Real World Cues: A New Look at Agenda-Setting by the Media." *American Journal of Political Science*, 24(1), 16–49.

Felstiner, W. L. F., Abeland, R. L., and Sarat, A. (1980). "The Emergence and Transformation of Disputes: Naming, Blaming, Claiming." *Law and Society Review*, 15(3–4), 631–54.

Fischer, F. (2003). *Reframing Public Policy: Discursive Politics and Deliberative Practices*. Oxford: Oxford University Press.

Hammond, T. H. (1986). "Agenda Control, Organizational Structure, and Bureaucratic Politics." *American Journal of Political Science*, 30(2), 379–420.

Hansford, T. G. (2004). "Lobbying Strategies, Venue Selection, and Organized Interest Involvement at the U.S. Supreme Court." *American Politics Research*, 32(2), 170–97.

Hisschemoller, M., and Hoppe, R. (1995). "Coping with Intractable Controversies: The Case for Problem Structuring in Policy Design and Analysis." *Knowledge and Policy*, 8(4), 40–61.

Howlett, M. (1998). "Predictable and Unpredictable Policy Windows: Issue, Institutional and Exogenous Correlates of Canadian Federal Agenda-Setting." *Canadian Journal of Political Science*, 31(3), 495–524.

Howlett, M. (September–December 2015). "Policy Analytical Capacity: The Supply and Demand for Policy Analysis in Government." *Policy and Society*, 34(3–4), 173–82 [accessed October 5, 2015].

Jones, B. D. (1994). *Re-Conceiving Decision-Making in Democratic Politics: Attention, Choice and Public Policy*. Chicago, IL: University of Chicago Press.

Kingdon, J. W. (1984). *Agendas, Alternatives, and Public Policies*. Boston, MA: Little Brown & Company.

Levin, K., Cashore, B., Bernstein, S., and Auld, G. (2012). "Overcoming the Tragedy of Super Wicked Problems: Constraining our Future Selves to Ameliorate Global Climate Change." *Policy Sciences*, 45(2), 123–52.

McFarland, A. S. (1987). "Interest Groups and Theories of Power in America." *British Journal of Political Science*, 17(2), 129–47.

Mukherjee, I. and Howlett, M. (August 2016). "Who Is a Stream? Epistemic Communities, Instrument Constituencies and Advocacy Coalitions in Public Policy-Making." *Politics and Governance*, 3(2), 65.

Peters, B. G. (2005). "The Problem of Policy Problems." *Journal of Comparative Policy Analysis: Research and Practice*, 7(4), 349–70.

Peters, B. G. (September–December 2016) "Organizational Political Capacity." *Policy and Society*, 34(3–4), 219–28.

Pritchard, D. (1992). *The News Media and Public Policy Agendas. Public Opinion, the Press, and Public Policy*, in J. D. Kennamer (Ed.), *Public Opinion, the Press, and Public Policy*. Westport, CT: Praeger, pp. 103–12.

Rittel, H. W. J. and Webber, M. M. (1973). "Dilemmas in a General Theory of Planning." *Policy Sciences*, 4, 155–69.

Rochefort, D. A. and Cobb, R. W. (1993). "Problem Definition, Agenda Access, and Policy Choice." *Policy Studies Journal*, 21(1), 56–71.

Rochefort, D. A. and Cobb, R. W. (1994). *The Politics of Problem Definition: Shaping the Policy Agenda*. Lawrence, KS: University of Kansas Press.

Rose, N. A. and Parsons, E. C. M. (October 2015). "'Back Off, Man, I'm a Scientist!' When Marine Conservation Science Meets Policy." *Ocean & Coastal Management, Making Marine Science Matter: Issues and Solutions from the 3rd International Marine Conservation Congress*, 115, 71–76.

Rosenbloom, D. (2008). "The Politics–Administration Dichotomy in US Historical Context." *Public Administration Review*, 68(1), 57–60.

Salisbury, R. H., Heinz, J. P., Laumann, E. O., and R. L. Nelson (1987). "Who Works with Whom? Interest Group Alliances and Opposition." *American Political Science Review* 81(4), 1217–34.

Saward, M. (1992). *Co-Optive Politics and State Legitimacy*. Aldershot: Dartmouth: OUP.

Schneider, A. L. and Ingram, H. (1997). *Policy Design for Democracy*. Lawrence, KS: University Press of Kansas.

Simon, H. A. (Winter 1973). "The Structure of Ill Structured Problems." *Artificial Intelligence*, 4(3–4), 181–201.

Skodvin, T., Gullberg A. T., and Aakre, S. (2010). "Target-Group Influence and Political Feasibility: The Case of Climate Policy Design in Europe." *Journal of European Public Policy*, 17(6), 854.

Sidney, M. S. (2007). "Policy Formulation: Design and Tools," in Fischer, F., Miller, G. J., and Sidney, M. S. (Eds.), *Handbook of Public Policy Analysis: Theory, Politics and Methods*. New Brunswick, NJ: CRC Taylor & Francis, pp. 79–87.

Stone, D. A. (1989). "Causal Stories and the Formation of Policy Agendas." *Political Science Quarterly*, 104(2), 281–300.

Stone, D. (2002). *Policy Paradox: The Art of Political Decision Making* (3rd edition). New York: Norton.

3 Policy formulation

The commitment of governments to tackling pressing policy problems such as corruption, environmental degradation, and poverty is often admirably strong. However, converting such commitment into measurable achievements requires that problems are defined correctly (see Chapter 2) and that appropriate measures are chosen and deployed to address them. In particular, the measures must be politically acceptable, administratively feasible, and technically sound, a tall order in the best of policy-making circumstances (Mukherjee and Howlett 2014).

Policy formulation refers to the process of generating a set of plausible policy choices capable of addressing problems identified during agenda-setting (Howlett et al. 2009). In this activity, a range of potential policy choices are identified and some preliminary assessments of their feasibility to resolve the identified problem are made. This can take place at the agenda-setting stage, as noted in Chapter 2, or indeed even before that stage as think tanks and government agencies envision and plan for a variety of alternative future scenarios they might face.

Policy formulation as conceptualized here is thus somewhat different from what is described in more linear depictions of the policy process. These depictions tend to restrict formulation activities to those that start only after a policy problem has entered the formal policy agenda and end after a range of options have been identified. Policy formulation, as we use the term here, extends throughout the policy process. The search for new policy options thus may precede the initiation of a policy problem in agenda-setting, but also may extend beyond the point where a decision is made and implemented to the evaluation of existing and future potential means to resolve public problems after a policy or program has been put into place (Sidney 2007).

The persistence (or worsening) of social, economic, and environmental problems in many countries unfortunately suggests that the ability of existing policy processes to generate acceptable policy options cannot be taken for granted. In some cases, alternatives that can meet the three criteria or political acceptability, administrative feasibility, and technically soundness simply may not exist. Governments may be faced with only a collection of poor alternative courses of action that fall down on one or more of these measures. In other cases, governments might fail to develop such options even where they could do so.

Policymakers may be pressured by policy community members—including actors from outside of government or in the international arena–to be confronted with an unappealing choice: selecting from among policy options that all suffer from noticeable deficiencies (such as being fundamentally unsuited to conditions on the ground, or differing only marginally from existing, underperforming policies), or undertaking no action at all (de Leon 1992).

This chapter provides an overview of the challenges governments confront in generating better policy options and how these barriers may be overcome. It addresses the roles public sector managers and other policy actors play in formulation, the constraints they face and the strategies they can adopt to enhance the effectiveness of their actions. The essential features and imperatives of policy formulation are set out, and why and how policy actors participate in this activity described. The last two sections then discuss the obstacles to better policy formulation and how they may be overcome through concerted efforts on the part of public sector managers.

The basics of policy formulation

What is policy formulation?

In general, the policy formulation process involves several tasks related to generation and assessment of options to address identified problems. The process can be either highly structured "design" or entirely *ad hoc* and meaningless non-design (Howlett and Mukherjee 2013). In the former case, policy formulation involves a distinct "design" process in which technical experts develop or construct options specifically intended to address particular kinds of problems in a largely logical and intentional way (Bobrow 2006). In the latter instance, we can speak of "non-design" processes in which the intentional and technical analytic component of policy design is entirely or largely missing (Linder and Peters 1990).

Certain capacities and capabilities on the part of governments and nongovernmental actors are required if policy alternatives are to be generated and assessed. In the case of design processes, for example, a high level of knowledge and information is required in order to identify and assess policy options based on evidence of "what works, when" (Jung and Nutley 2008).

Determinants of the capacity to undertake rigorous policy evaluation include (Howlett 2009):

- availability of capable individual analysts;
- provisions for the collection and dissemination of relevant information;
- mechanisms to ensure access by agencies, nongovernmental organizations and the public to this information;
- social demand and support for evidence-based policy-making.

For policy formulation processes that are more politically driven, policy evidence may itself be far less relevant, but other specific kinds of governing capabilities and competences in areas related to political decision-making—such as the ability to legitimize non-technical and often partisan processes and to construct and execute acceptable political bargains—will feature more prominently.

Although new circumstances may propel the creation of new packages of policy solutions, this is rarely the case. Rather, options and alternatives are typically developed where historical circumstances or "policy legacies" condition what can be done and by whom (Weir 1992). Initiatives are then "layered" onto already existing older ones (Van der Heijden 2011; Thelen 2004) and formulation proceeds more through a process of "patching" an old regime rather than "packaging" a new one (Howlett and Rayner 2013). New or revised tools and mechanisms are proposed that add to existing ones, like software patches intended to correct problems encountered in the use of older platforms. In some cases, this may involve "stretching" existing elements—such as enlarging subsidies or tax breaks or enhancing fines and penalties—to cover disappointing results. In others, it may include adding new elements to an existing policy mix—like a tax break or loan to support an industrial sector that the government previously had always supported through cash subsidies or grants (Feindt and Flynn 2009).

Phases in policy formulation

Policy formulation will by definition involve government analysts and advisors, but in most cases, it will also involve a variety of nongovernmental advisors (Waller 1992; Bakvis 1997). These different actors from the policy community make up the components of a "policy advice" or "policy advisory system" whose membership will vary from issue to issue and government to government but whose general contours and structure typically remain more or less fixed institutionally or in practice (Craft and Howlett 2012).

Most influential actors in policy formulation are commonly those closest to the government either geographically or ideologically. But this is not

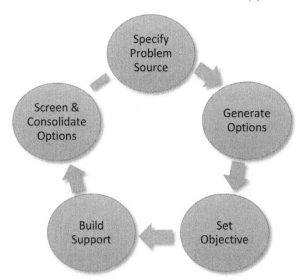

Figure 3.1 Policy formulation process

always the case; sometimes relatively peripheral actors—such as aid donors or military allies in many developing countries—can exercise a disproportionate influence over policy formulation. In many countries, fairly closed advisory systems centered on government ministries and agencies have opened up in recent years to incorporate greater stakeholder consultation and public participation (Prince 2007). This has often been accompanied by a downgrading of technical analysis in favor of more political sources of opinion, expertise, and advice (Craft and Howlett 2013).

Specifying the source of the problem

The policy formulation process begins with debates and consideration among various actors about the actual sources and causes of a problem that the government has to address (Thomas 2001). In some cases, it may be concluded that a problem is more of a condition or circumstance that cannot be resolved, leading to a recommendation either to accept the *status quo* or to engage in some symbolic activities aimed at recognizing the seriousness of the condition while signaling that little will or can be done about it. Presidential speeches at funerals of mass shooting victims in the US are a good example of the latter activity.

Normally, however, there do exist one or more sources of the problem that can be identified and understood so that it can be targeted for resolution through policy intervention. The identified source of the problem needs to be based not only on evidence and logic but also must be practical in the sense that something can be done about it. For instance, it may well be true that venal intention on the part of many individuals is the root cause of high crime rate but it is not a useful insight for policy actors because there is little they can do about it. On the other hand, sources such as deprivation, unfavorable family upbringing, weak law and order situation, and so on are possible problem sources which policymakers can indeed address.

Getting to the root causes of the problem and specifying them precisely and practically are hard work and frequently avoided. It is far easier for policy actors to simply appeal to our fears, prejudices, and ideologies in specifying causes. If this happens, it is unlikely that effective solutions will emerge. As Albert Einstein is believed to have famously said: "If I had only one hour to save the world, I would spend fifty-five minutes defining the problem, and only five minutes finding the solution." Once the problem and its sources have been understood, the possible solutions would likely be staring at us.

Generating policy options

The second phase of the formulation process involves an assessment of what tools for dealing with a particular problem are available for deployment. This can involve both an abstract discussion of the tools that could *logically* address a problem, and/or a more detailed assessment of the resources—funding, personnel, knowledge, and authority—governments can bring to bear on a problem at the time when action is expected to occur (Anderson 1977; Hood 1986).

As Table 3.1 shows, policies are comprised of a number of elements that must be aligned if they are to succeed (Howlett 2009a). These include several levels of goals—from the most abstract to the operational—as well as a range of means, from general preferences for governing arrangements to the exact specification of the size of a subsidy or fine to be levied in a particular circumstance and the kinds of resources dedicated to their operation (Howlett and Cashore 2007 and 2009).

As this table illustrates, when policy actors are exploring policy options, they must consider not only *what* to do but also *how* to do it. While formulating a policy to tackle traffic congestion, for example, policy actors must simultaneously consider whether to build more roads, improve public transport, restrict automobile usage, or deploy some combination of these as well as the tools by which the policy will actually be implemented and the sequence in which they will be deployed. These *policy tools*, also known as *policy instruments* or *governing instruments*, are the actual means or devices

Table 3.1 Components of a public policy

		POLICY CONTENT		
		High level abstraction	*Program level operationalization*	*Specific measures*
POLICY FOCUS	Policy aims	GOALS What general types of ideas govern policy development? E.g. environmental protection, economic growth.	OBJECTIVES What does policy formally aim to address? E.g. saving wilderness or species habitat, increasing harvesting levels to create processing jobs.	SETTINGS What are the specific on-the-ground requirements of a policy? E.g. considerations about sustainable levels of harvesting.
	Policy means or tools	INSTRUMENT LOGIC What general norms guide implementation preferences? E.g. preferences for the use of coercive instruments, or moral suasion.	TOOLS What specific types of instruments are utilized? E.g. the use of different tools such as tax incentives, or regulations.	RESOURCES What kinds of personnel and funding are allocated to operate the selected tools?

Source: Howlett and Cashore 2009

that governments use to implement policies. Each policy tool considered to resolve a problem is a concrete mechanism for achieving a policy goal. Policy formulation in this sense is about finding and deploying the right tools for achieving specific purposes.

It is possible to classify policy tools and instruments into a relatively small number of specific types (though these have countless variations and combinations in practice) and to say something about the modalities and requirements of tools in each category. Policy tools may be divided into two main categories, private and public, depending on the extent to which they rely on private resources or public authority for their effectiveness (see Table 3.2). There are also hybrid and mixed tools—co-production, co-design etc.—that mix and match private and public instruments, resources and capabilities.

Private instruments usually involve little or no direct government activity or participation on the basis of the belief that a solution is or will be provided more efficiently and/or effectively by private actors alone. The key forms of private tools are market, family, and voluntary social organizations. When these tools are employed, the desired task is typically performed on a largely voluntary basis by private agents, who may be motivated by financial rewards, emotional satisfaction, religious inspiration, or ideology.

Table 3.2 Examples of policy tools

Private tools	Mixed	Public tools
• Market • Voluntary organizations • Family	• Collaborative tools such as co-design, co-production, and co-management	• Information, suasion, nudges • Economic incentives and disincentives • Regulations • State enterprises • Direct provision

Exactly how this may come about and what kinds of goods or services may be provided by what kind of group—family, religious organizations, charities, private firms, and so on—will vary according to the group's motivation, and policy formulators proposing the use of private tools must be aware of the limits and capabilities of the group (Howlett et al. 2009).

However, it is more common for private instruments to be backed by varying levels of indirect government involvement than to be exercised solely by private actors. Thus, governments not only uphold property rights and enforce contracts—tasks that are essential for markets to work—but they also offer various kinds of subsidies to help shape market behavior and push it in their preferred direction. Similarly, governments provide subsidies and information to help make families and voluntary organizations operate in the manner they desire.

The same is true of various forms of collaboration such as co-production, co-design, and co-management of public policies. These are true hybrid forms of organization in which governmental and nongovernmental actors are both active. A good example of such arrangements is parent-teacher associations which mobilize parents in support of public, and sometimes private, educational programs (Pestoff 2006 and Pestoff et al. 2012).

Public instruments, on the other hand, are much more direct in terms of service provision or their impact on other actors (Salamon 2002). They are backed by state sovereignty and/or information that resides within governments; and they are directed by policymakers toward certain types of activities, linked to the expected resolution of policy problems. Thus, governments may:

- employ taxes, regulations, or jail sentences and fines to discourage undesired behavior;
- launch public enterprises to pursue social and economic goals simultaneously;

- provide subsidies to promote desired behavior;
- engage in manipulation of conscious and sub-conscious behaviors (the so-called "nudge" approach in public policy design) in order to promote desired goals, such as weight loss or tobacco control.

Often, multiple instruments are deployed simultaneously. In the area of environment protection, one may find the government providing subsidies to promote the use of clean technology, taxing unclean technology, providing information to park users about animals and trails, and engaging in various kinds of advertising and placement of recycling barrels or other such "nudges" aimed at preventing or discouraging littering (Thaler and Sunstein 2009).

The use of regulations is particularly widespread in controlling economic activities, whereas state enterprises and direct provision are used mostly for providing specific kinds of social goods and services, from public roads to military equipment and defense. The government is also a repository of vast amounts of information that it can use to promote desired behavior (for example, promoting water conservation in arid countries) and avoid undesired behavior (for example, discouraging smoking, obesity, unsafe sex, or other health-related issues) through educating, persuading, or nudging individuals and groups (Hood 1986).

Each generic tool category has its own dynamics and operating characteristics, which lead to some predictable consequences of their use (Salamon 2002). Even so, many unanticipated effects may become apparent during the course of implementation, some arising from unfamiliarity with particular tools on the part of policy actors. It should also be recognized that there is a degree of substitutability among tools, meaning that sometimes different tools can be employed to achieve the same end; for example, one can use a government agency to provide telecommunications service, build infrastructure, or to provide tax breaks and subsidies to private firms to do the same thing. Other complexities arise simply from the fact that tools are typically used in conjunction with others in a "policy mix," whose interactive effects are difficult to predict and control (del Rio 2013). It should also be recalled that although it may be couched in more or less neutral, technical terms, the choice of instrument is as much a political matter as a technical one. After all, the deployment of different instruments affects different groups differently.

Good design thus requires:

- knowledge of the underlying problems and their severity;
- an understanding of the features of various tools;
- grasp of the effects of different tools on policy targets;

- the application of that knowledge to the development of policies aimed at achieving policy goals; and
- the ability to estimate the resources necessary for deploying the tools and the *ex ante* evaluation of the policy options against some accepted criteria (e.g. effectiveness, efficiency, equity) (Howlett et al. 2014).

Both imagination and judgment are often essential due to the need to formulate policy in situations often characterized by lack of time and information, preventing the use of alternative trial-and-error learning strategies such as the use of policy pilots or experiments to gauge policy and impacts (Nair and Howlett 2016). Activities which are not design-oriented also require knowledge of policy tools and their impacts but with even more weight given to political impacts rather than technical considerations. Governing arrangements, however, often exist as a stock of typical solutions that may serve as starting points in formulation discussions and advice-giving. For example, different actors, policy networks, or governance contexts may have a marked preference for market, legal, network, or corporatist types of policy mechanisms. Policy formulators are also able to draw on examples of the successful (and failed) use of particular tools or mixes in other governing contexts or countries (Considine and Lewis 2003).

Setting objectives

A key activity in the policy formulation stage consists of setting the specific objectives that the government seeks to achieve in deploying any particular policy tool and ensuring they are adequately resourced and operationalized. While this may sound self-evident, governments are often unclear about what exactly they seek to achieve through a policy. For example, if the policy aim is to reduce poverty, questions arise such as "by how much" and "among which group"? Reduction to zero in all groups requires a different response than reduction by only a small percentage in a group such as the elderly or among single mothers. And at what speed should this occur? Over a month or a decade? Different problems have different imperatives, and the tempo of change required or anticipated is an important factor in deciding how to address them, and which tools to use, in what sequence, in order to do so (Justen et al. 2013).

A useful way to think about the nature of the options developed in the policy formulation process is to frame them in terms of the extent to which they depart from the *status quo*. Policy alternatives can be categorized into two types based on this criterion: incremental alternatives and non-incremental alternatives. *Incremental alternatives*, as the name suggests, are policy alternatives that are only marginally different from what is already in place, while *non-incremental alternatives* represent a significant departure from the status quo in terms of the ideas they embody, the interests they serve, and the policy instruments they propose (Lindblom 1959). *Policy innovations* may exist in either case. They may consist of developing something entirely new or useful or, as is more common, employing existing practices, arrangements, or tools in new ways for new uses. The innovative use of policy tools by borrowing from their use in other sectors or contexts is often a particularly fruitful device employed by those looking for new ideas and new ways to deal with problems (Polsby 1984). One such instance is Singapore's use of the auction of ownership rights to curb the purchase of cars, a practice borrowed from the environment sector where pollution rights are auctioned to firms in polluting industries. Another example is the imposition of fossil fuel taxes coupled with the removal of employment-related taxes; these can simultaneously address the problems of carbon emissions and unemployment without affecting the government's overall finances. Partnerships with the private sector may also improve services without raising costs. Again, however, policy actors require experience, expert researchers, and other forms of policy capacity in order to develop feasible innovations based on the experiences of other countries or contexts for the application of the tools (Painter and Pierre 2005).

Although innovations entailing fundamental changes may occur, there is a strong tendency for policymakers to search mainly for incremental alternatives in policy formulation. This is so for several reasons. First, fundamental overhauls require multiple changes to existing policies and information on the likely impact of such changes is more difficult to obtain than that based on existing experiences. It is also the case that incremental alternatives consume fewer resources, because financial, personnel, and organizational arrangements are often already in place and only need to be marginally "tweaked" to implement proposed changes. As a result, many possible alternatives are likely to be set aside on the grounds that they are "unproven" or lack evidence of their efficacy. Enacting non-incremental alternatives also involves a higher risk for many policymakers because of greater uncertainties and, as a result, the higher degree of risk they entail for budgets, society, political and administrative reputations, and job prospects if something should go wrong. Finally, the characteristics of large, complex organizations—fragmentation, inertia, red tape, routines, and conflicting goals—tend to be strongly biased toward the preservation of the *status quo* (Hayes 1992).

This bias toward incremental alternatives has significant implications for policy-making. It can prevent or inhibit the consideration of new solutions to problems even when there is a pressing need for a new course of action. In contemporary areas of concern, such as energy and climate change, for instance, substantial and dramatic changes may be necessary to reverse current trends, requiring policymakers to look in new directions rather than rework existing practices (Massey et al. 2014). But this is very difficult to achieve without managerial interventions and leadership.

Screening and consolidation of options

Once criteria or objectives have been set—however vague or diffuse they may be—the alternative combinations of instruments identified earlier can be assessed and compared in terms of how well they are likely to achieve these goals and at what cost. The purpose of this assessment is to draw conclusions about the attractiveness of alternative options against set criteria and to provide some sort of estimation about the relative costs and efficiency, both technical and political, involved in their adoption. In this way, policy actors can make an informed choice (Harrington and Morgenstern 2004).

The most fundamental test is whether or not the specific option is effective, i.e. if it addresses the source of the problem identified in agenda-setting. Hence, for example, the use of tax breaks or incentives for attracting foreign investment would be useful only if a high tax is thought to be the main barrier to investment. Other criteria for assessment may include efficiency, equity, political and administrative feasibility, and sustainability.

These assessments and comparisons of policy options may be technical or political. Technical analysis typically involves the use of formal analytical tools and techniques for assessing different aspects of policy choices such as cost-benefit analysis or cost-effectiveness studies (among many other techniques). But technical assessment of policy options is difficult. Insufficient information on the problems, or on the effects of policy tools, may lead to unreliable or misleading conclusions. Many policy issues involve value judgments not amenable to technical analysis. As a result, analysts often concentrate only on the criteria of cost-effectiveness, which they measure in terms of how much impact is gained at what cost. But costs, and especially benefits, are often hard to estimate and techniques such as cost-benefit analysis may not provide as much guidance into tool choice and program design as is hoped. The benefits of spending public money on promoting a national language or building an opera hall, for example, involve intangible cultural benefits that cannot be calculated with any degree of precision—but that also cannot be left out of alternative appraisal and evaluation.

More reflexive assessment is thus common and is based on the assessor's own experience and judgment and can be undertaken in conjunction with or in lieu of technical assessment. Such assessments may be useful, but are usually skewed towards the *status quo*. Such assessments can also be done systematically through meetings and deliberations for the purpose of collaborative or participatory co-design—such as public hearings or design charrettes—that can transcend some of these limitations. Such design mechanisms have their own difficulties and sensitive political considerations, however—such as determining who to invite to attend, where deliberations will be held and under what rules, and for how long and at what cost.

Consulting and building support

After making a preliminary assessment of the pros and cons of specific alternatives to resolve a problem, it is common for some processes to then unfold either within the government or outside in the policy community to legitimize and gather support for a small set of options that can be brought forward to decision-makers for their selection and approval (Bryson et al. 2002). This often involves formal or informal consultation with stakeholders in order to gain further insight into the alternatives, to educate stakeholders about the nature of the problems and the proposed solutions, and to build support for the policy formulation process followed and the alternatives that will result from it. Arnold Meltsner (1972) has developed a useful checklist for managers to use to assess the political acceptability of different policy alternatives. *Who* are the relevant actors? *What* are their motivations and beliefs? *What* are their political resources? *In which* political arenas will the relevant decisions be made?

A feasible policy choice must be politically acceptable—or at least not patently unacceptable to affected members of policy communities and governments (Majone 1975). Thus, many otherwise perfectly fine policy options may be infeasible because, for example, they would be unacceptable to the affected parties whose support is necessary to legitimize government action, or because the political support needed to authorize and fund policy implementation is not in place and could under no foreseeable circumstances be mobilized.

While it is important to screen out infeasible policy choices in the short term, one should not take a static view of feasibility. New policy choices may emerge during the screening process. For example, someone may realize that certain features of an alternative increase the cost disproportionately to their contribution to effectiveness, leading to a search for alternatives that are equally effective but less costly. Similarly, new features may be found to increase effectiveness with little added cost (Freed et al. 2002).

And what may have been infeasible in the past may be feasible today or in the future. Political circumstances, social pressures, available technologies, and the understanding and framing of problems themselves all change over time. What may be impossible at one point in time may be possible later.

Think of the situation following the election of a new government with new personalities, agendas, goals, and instrument preferences which may open the door for policy considered infeasible not long ago. Many of the environmental protection measures adopted recently, for instance, such as carbon taxes, were not thinkable even a decade ago, before concerns with phenomena such as global warming arose on the policy agenda. Surprises can work in all directions: the scrapping of many environmental regulations—and even of anti-climate change policies—that has been promised by the incoming Trump administration in the US also has no precedent among major countries.

Options that are believed to be unworkable or unacceptable to stakeholders are eliminated during the process of consultation. If no workable and acceptable option is found after consultation, the search for policy alternatives restarts. However, more typically, the result is the consolidation or the restriction of alternatives to a few plausible working solutions which can be forwarded to the decision-makers for further consideration. In many instances this may mean presentation of only a single option; but in others, two or more may survive the acid test of political feasibility (alongside other salient criteria) to be presented (Öberg et al. 2015).

The end result of the formulation process, which can be either lengthy or short, is a relatively small number of reasonably well-articulated technically and/or politically acceptable alternative options to address problems on the decision agenda (Bardach 2000). These remaining alternatives are often summarized in a (typically short) document—such as a Memorandum to Cabinet or a ministerial policy brief—which can be submitted to decision-makers describing the recommendation and laying out its strengths and demerits against key criteria specific to the context at hand (such as ensuring harmonious federal-provincial relations, or ensuring that consultation with affected groups has taken place satisfactorily).

Challenges in policy formulation

As has been suggested above, there are many challenges that policy actors and advisors face in policy formulation activities. These include problems ranging from fiscal constraints (that might not allow consideration of a preferred subsidy scheme for high-tech industries, for example) to considerations about elections and other political events that can make the timing of the formulation process and its unfolding problematical for the government of the day. Technically viable options may fall by the wayside if the government senses that opposition groups and parties, for example, would use them to mobilize those who would be adversely affected by the proposals (Colebatch and Radin 2006).

Such challenges can combine to result in formulation processes that fail to develop or propose alternatives that can effectively and efficiently deal with the problem at hand. (As we shall see, many of these challenges can be overcome through government action, however.) Challenges to policy formulation can be categorized according to whether they are political, technical, or organizational in nature and whether their resolution involves capacity-building in these particular areas (James and Jorgensen 2009).

Political challenges

As we have seen, the political environment is not always conducive to systematic policy formulation and the consideration of a wide range of policy options. Often senior government officials at the top of the policy pyramid do not know exactly what they want, and will only form ideas in a general way—for example the need for improved access to safe drinking water or the promotion of economic development in a depressed region. At other times, they may say things they do not really mean. For example, they may express their commitment to poverty eradication through greater public spending while avoiding the imposition of additional taxes that might decrease their electoral prospects. In such situations, policy actors may be at a loss to fathom what cues to read in order to formulate appropriate policy options (Macrae and Whittington 1997).

Even when political masters know which problems they want to address and express their views transparently, the public may not be supportive of the possible solutions mooted. People dislike traffic congestion in urban areas, for example, but they dislike most solutions even more: public transport, because it is inconvenient; more roads, because they could mean more taxes; and the pricing of road use (such as additional charges for licensing, fuel, peak hour road use, or parking), because it is both expensive and inconvenient. To complicate the situation, local residents want to continue to use personal cars while wanting controls against non-resident traffic. This potential public opposition to possible measures to ease traffic congestion is distinct from the opposition of other organs of the government itself. The government agency in charge of small business development, for example, may actually want *more* cars coming into a downtown core to enhance patronage of local business by well-heeled suburban consumers. In contrast, an environment agency concerned about the pollution caused by vehicular traffic would be likely to advocate just the opposite (Montpetit 2003).

The nature and composition of the policy community may also pose political challenges for policy formulation. Some communities are "closed" in that they allow neither new actors nor new ideas to penetrate into the community. In such instances, any option involving major changes will not be seriously entertained. The existence of powerful professional and business groups—physicians, insurers, and pharmaceutical firms in the health care sector, for instance—and their entrenched interests and ideas also cast an indirect but pervasive shadow over the formulation process and can limit the range of alternatives actively considered (such as limiting the possibility of the creation of a national health system in the US and other countries). Policy advisors must be aware of the implications of closed policy communities and powerful groups and be prepared to work with or around them (Bardach 2000).

Technical challenges

Despite the priority frequently given to overcoming *political* obstacles, it is often the *technical* barriers that can be most challenging in policy formulation. The difficulties start with understanding the cause of the problem being addressed and the objectives being sought in order to consolidate and scrutinize specific policy options capable of addressing these concerns.

In this regard, when formulating policies, policy formulators are faced with numerous *substantive* constraints. If there is a lack of a common understanding of the sources of a policy problem and no way to determine which of the many possible competing interpretations is correct, policy actors will find it hard to recognize which objectives to pursue, where to look for alternatives, or what criteria to use to sift or sort policy options. Even when a problem is very narrowly defined— for example, poverty can most simply be defined as a lack of sufficient monetary income—their hands may be tied with respect to the available options. Simply printing more money and distributing it to the poor is inadvisable because the inflation that will result from such an increase in the money supply will offset any gains in income. So, one must necessarily address the problem in more complicated ways. Similarly, the problem of global warming cannot be entirely eliminated in the near future because, as yet, there is no known solution to carbon and other greenhouse gas emissions that can be deployed without causing large-scale economic and social disruption in the short term. All of these limitations point to intractability in the technical characteristics of many policy problems.

As a result of these and other substantive constraints, policy actors often have to consider a wide range of policy options, many with little or no potential for success, in order to identify measures that might make a net improvement to a situation (Lester and Stewart 2000). While the experience of policy actors and their agencies in any one policy sector is an asset in providing information about past efforts to deal with any particular problem, the same experience can also be a barrier to formulating creative options. The current situation may appear normal and in need of only minor improvement, with the result that a proposal for substantial changes might well appear to be an unnecessary aberration.

Organizational and operational challenges

Operational constraints also exist for effective policy formulation. These have to do with deep-rooted features of the surrounding context that make it difficult to adopt particular policy options or put them into effect. They can take many different forms. Constitutional provisions and the political system form a vital constraint that can limit the range of options available in a given situation. Efforts to control handguns in the US, for example, immediately come up against the constitutional right of citizens to bear arms. The existence of two or more levels of government in federal systems imposes similar constraints because many national policies require inter-governmental agreement, something that can be impossible or very time-consuming to obtain. The electoral system can also serve to determine a government's "policy horizons," the effect of which may be to limit the kinds of policy options that can be considered feasible for electoral or political reasons (Warwick 2000).

Standard operating procedures in bureaucratic agencies also pose a major institutional barrier to policy formation (Bardach 2000). While set procedures are vital for upholding the principles of accountability and promoting predictability, they form a barrier to the search for integration and policy innovation. Segmentation of policy authority along sectoral lines, too, poses a hurdle to achieving integration in policy formulation. There is a tendency for each agency to de-emphasize the goals and alternatives that lie outside its immediate domain while promoting its own role. This is a problem because policy problems do not respect sectoral or organizational boundaries and solutions may well, and typically do, transcend such borders.

Strategies to improve policy formulation

There are numerous ways in which policy actors can enhance their role in policy formulation. One very important activity they can undertake is to collect *in advance* the necessary information on various aspects of emerging and existing problems and develop solutions for use by policymakers when the need arises (Hsu 2016). Managers in government agencies have a special advantage in this role: most policy proposals involve modification of existing policies or programs, with which the public managers are very familiar from their implementation experience. Public managers, especially those with formal training in public policy, are particularly well equipped to ensure that technical issues are given due consideration in policy formulation and to ensure that they are in a position to do so by undertaking early and systematic collection of evidence (Howlett and Wellstead 2011). Nevertheless, it is often difficult for public managers to play a proactive role in policy formulation. As mentioned above, the lack of understanding of the causes of the problem being addressed surprisingly common in the formulation stage. Ambitious efforts to prepare for and participate in policy formulation can prove to be fruitless or worse. Depending on the way in which their performance is evaluated, contributions to policy formulation may not benefit and indeed may even hurt public managers' career prospects if they are not equally sensitive to the priorities of powerful actors both within government and also outside it. Moreover, public managers' early involvement in policy formulation carries a danger of being perceived as merely advancing the interests of the agencies they represent. The fragmentation of the policy process across various agencies and layers often only aggravates the problem that proactive agencies may be viewed, correctly or not, as merely guarding their "turf."

Public managers thus need to make special efforts to overcome the difficulties and challenges that hinder their policy formulation efforts. First, they may want to leverage their access to information on existing policies and programs to contribute to the early analysis of reform proposals. The fact that they have implementation experience in the area and that most policy proposals seek only small changes to existing policies works in their favor. Moreover, to bolster their policy capacity, they may need to hire outside experts on the policy issue at hand. Tapping into relevant policy networks can also be useful in making a meaningful contribution to policy formation. All these strategies help to counter the view that their behavior is purely self-interested (Pal and Clark 2016).

While difficult, there are several strategies which policy managers and other policy actors can adopt to improve their input into and the outputs of the policy formulation process.

Better understanding of the source of the problem

While studying the root causes of the problem in question is not the purpose of policy formulation, it cannot be avoided. Which options have a fighting chance of being effective depends substantially on what actually caused the problem in the first place. However, often there can be many different interpretations of the causes of problems with no definite means to determine their validity. Some policy problems are so complex—think of poverty or banking crises—that there will probably never be full agreement over their true underlying causes; yet policymakers must do *something* about them. Policymakers typically respond by selecting a *plausible* interpretation of the source of the problem and then moving on to doing something about it. In some quarters the need to pinpoint the causes continues to be strongly emphasized. The United Nations Common Country Assessment (CCA), for instance, requires analysis that identifies the immediate, underlying, and root causes of the problems. While this is desirable, it is not possible in many instances, despite the availability of various tools for causality analysis. Thus, while we can identify the different levels of causes of traffic congestion and housing shortages, despite their complexities, it is unlikely that we will ever identify the causes of poverty or school underperformance that will be accepted by all concerned. But, in general, the stronger the evidence on which policy formulation rests, the greater the likelihood of policy success (Nutley et al. 2007).

Better clarification of policy objectives

Another problem facing policy formulators is that in order to consider and appraise options, they need to have a clear sense of the goals they are expected to achieve, and on what time line. While the political executive typically has the primary responsibility for setting overall objectives, these are often too broad to be applied precisely to specific problem contexts. The task of fleshing out the objectives falls on those involved in policy formulation. For example, the goal of reducing global warming must be translated into something more specific, such as reducing carbon emissions. But even this is too broad for operational purposes. It often falls on policy formulators to clarify operational objectives so that they can then devise the means to achieve them (Noordegraaf 2000). What the exact level of tax and/or subsidy would be is a task for decision-making, but various options can still be developed at this stage and their potential consequences laid out for decision-makers.

Broadening the sources for generating policy alternatives

One of the biggest problems in policy formulation is the narrow search for policy alternatives, centered around existing practices. As mentioned earlier, this is often the result of closed policy communities whose interest lie in preserving the *status quo* or expanding the benefits to themselves and excluding others. Reconfiguring and opening up the policy community would be the optimal solution, one that may be achieved simply by introducing new members with new ideas. Policymakers may consider, for example, including representatives from mainstream environmental groups in the advisory system associated with the mining industry to make the latter more sensitive to environmental concerns.

Even in the absence of new actors, a broader range of meaningful alternatives may emerge from a variety of sources, including policy modeling and policy transfer.

One way to generate options is to *model the problem* by identifying probable causes. For example, the problem of deforestation can be modelled by looking at several plausible causes that can be influenced by policy intervention. These causes can be categorized into five groups:

1. poor governance;
2. insufficient attention to the local community;
3. poor consultation processes;
4. limited or conflicting information; and
5. problems with existing laws and regulations.

Within each of the probable causes lies a possible solution. Thus, if poor governance is believed to be the key problem, then the answer possibly lies in strengthening governance in the forestry sector. However, the modelling of problems does not necessarily lead to the generation of specific policy options. Rather, it helps to identify the "intervening variables" that the policy options might be designed to affect. It is risky to leap from an "intervening variable" to a single policy proposal, because the policy proposed may not achieve the required change for the variable, or it could even cause a whole new set of problems to emerge.

Policy options can also be generated by learning from policies used elsewhere, through *policy transfer*. This process is sometimes also referred to as "borrowing" and "tinkering" (Weimer 1993). For example, the use of economic incentives in environmental protection policies that originated in the West has been transferred to many developing countries in dealing with their environmental challenges. Privatization and deregulation of telecommunications in the UK and civil aviation in the US in the early 1980s were both widely emulated in other countries in subsequent years (Howlett and Ramesh 1993). The challenges for sustainable development are remarkably similar in many countries, for example, and there are increased opportunities to "learn" from experiences of policy interventions elsewhere. A technique as simple as searching the internet is currently one of the most widely used practices among policymakers seeking to ascertain what is being done about any given problem in other jurisdictions. Other more formal mechanisms also exist for this purpose—for example, international organizations such as the OECD, the IMF, and the World Bank have invested heavily in the development of knowledge hubs to fostering policy learning across countries and sectors.

Knowledge of foreign and other practices, however, may not always be readily available for policy actors to access and innovate upon. Again, early work and continual environmental scans on the part of prudent managers may prove invaluable in this regard.

Anticipating changes better and building political support

Given different and contradictory cues from the political environment, policy actors must tread carefully if they are to do their job professionally and effectively. While the lack of clarity or even honesty on the part of the political executive may be a problem, there is little individual policy actors can do to address this. What they can do is to seek as great a degree of transparency as possible, sometimes by clarifying pronouncements on their own and then seeking support for their interpretations.

Once they have arrived at a working interpretation of the sources of the problem and the objectives being sought in addressing it, they need to take additional steps to appreciate the political environment. It is in their professional and personal interest to read the political "winds" while analyzing and reporting possible policy solutions. Thus, while they should consider all plausible solutions fairly, it would be wise to give the most thorough attention to the strengths and weaknesses of the options known to be favored by their political masters (Pal and Clark 2016). It is also sensible to give the same attention to the options proposed by the main opposition party or by groups that may take office or enjoy the more sympathetic ear of government one day in the future. Anticipating and addressing the main lines of concern of various powerful stakeholders is essential. Formal and informal consultation, not only with stakeholders but also with the broader policy network and community, helps effective policy formulation. It not only elicits additional information and insights, but also helps policy actors build support for their analysis and recommendations (Pal and Clark 2016; Tiernan 2015).

Interagency committees or task forces can also help with effective policy formulation, especially when a problem may be the responsibility of one agency but has implications for many others with enough power collectively to stall the proposal during decision-making or implementation. Setting up interministerial committees or task forces to deal with foreign direct investments, for example, helps to formulate policies that can potentially incorporate the interests and objectives of different government agencies. Policy-makers can create processes for representing groups or resolving disputes—by appointing a committee, calling in a mediator, seeking to change the power balance by creating an independent commission, or changing the powers and resources enjoyed by certain key players (Marier 2008 and 2009). Widespread consultation may, however, also generate additional problems that need to be addressed. It can be time-consuming, and can also create opportunities for new lines of opposition to emerge. Policy actors have to make their own assessment, based on their experience, as to how much time they can realistically allocate to consultations when faced with deadlines. As a rule of thumb, however, they should err on the side of more consultation rather than less, not least because in this way potential opposition may surface earlier, giving them more time to respond and adjust policy formulation accordingly.

Leveraging on policy communities and networks

Policy actors may personally or collectively only be familiar with a limited range of possible options and the tools required for putting them into effect. This makes it difficult for them to recommend new or innovative options and tools. Better research and hiring of experienced and well-trained analysts are both essential for overcoming this problem. Commissioning outside consultants to recommend policy options is another alternative (Boston 1994).

Consultation with other members of the policy community is an inexpensive way to overcome technical challenges. Such consultations allow policy actors to understand the depth and breadth of the problem as well as the urgency with which it needs to be addressed. The various relevant interest groups, policymakers, and researchers often have an extensive knowledge of policy problems and potential solutions, which can offer a valuable source of information and insight. Consultations can also generate information on the lines and depth of opposition to, and support for, particular policy options being considered, enabling policy actors to accommodate and respond to the reservations expressed (Hendriks 2009).

Conclusion: the need for analytical capacity

Policy formulation is a key stage of policy-making and one in which policy actors and advisors may find their greatest opportunity to affect decision-making and policy implementation. It is a complex function involving a range of actors with different ideas about and different interests in the promotion of specific solutions to policy problems (Colebatch 2006). Policy-makers need to ensure that their advisors have the appropriate capacity, especially analytical capacity, to adequately carry out the many tasks involved in policy design and appraisal (Howlett 2016). Once this is done, however, they can be more confident that the proposals that come to them in the decision-making stage for adjudication and decision will be capable of "doing the job" and will not make a situation worse. It is to this decision-making activity that we now turn.

References

Anderson, C. W. (1977). *Statecraft: An Introduction to Political Choice and Judgement.* New York: John Wiley and Sons.

Anderson, G. (1996). "The New Focus on the Policy Capacity of the Federal Government." *Canadian Public Administration,* 39(4), 469–88.

Bakvis, H. (1997). "Advising the Executive: Think Tanks, Consultants, Political Staff and Kitchen Cabinets," in Weller, P., Bakvis, H., and Rhodes, R. A. W. (Eds.), *The Hollow Crown: Countervailing Trends in Core Executives.* New York: St. Martin's Press, pp. 84–125.

Bardach, E. (2000). *A Practical Guide for Policy Analysis: The Eightfold Path to More Effective Problem Solving.* New York: Chatham House Publishers.

Bobrow, D. (2006). "Policy Design: Ubiquitous, Necessary and Difficult," in Peters, B. G. and Pierre, J. (Eds), *Handbook of Public Policy.* Beverly Hills, CA: SAGE, pp. 75–96.

Boston, J. (1994). "Purchasing Policy Advice: The Limits of Contracting Out." *Governance,* 7(1), 1–30.

Bryson, J. M., Cunningham, G. L., and Lakkemoe, K. J. (2002). "What to Do When Stakeholders Matter: The Case of Problem Formulation for the African American Men Project of Hennepin County, Minnesota." *Public Administration Review,* 62(5), 568–84.

Colebatch, H. K. (November 2006). "What Work Makes Policy?" *Policy Sciences,* 39(4), 309–21. doi:10.1007/s11077–006–9025–4.

Colebatch, H. K. and Radin, B. A. (2006). "Mapping the Work of Policy," in H. K. Colebatch (Ed.), *The Work of Policy: An International Survey.* New York: Rowman & Littlefield, pp. 217–26.

Considine, M. and Lewis, J. M. (2003). "Bureaucracy, Network, or Enterprise? Comparing Models of Governance in Australia, Britain, the Netherlands, and New Zealand." *Public Administration Review,* 63(2), 131–40.

Craft, J. and Howlett, M. (2012). "Policy Formulation, Governance Shifts and Policy Influence: Location and Content in Policy Advisory Systems." *Journal of Public Policy,* 32(2), 79–98.

——— (September 2013). "The Dual Dynamics of Policy Advisory Systems: The Impact of Externalization and Politicization on Policy Advice." *Policy and Society, Externalization and Politicization of Policy Advice Systems,* 32(3), 187–97.

DeLeon, P. (1992). "Policy Formulation: Where Ignorant Armies Clash by Night." *Policy Studies Review,* 11(3/4), 389–405.

Del Río, P. (October 2013). "On Evaluating Success in Complex Policy Mixes: The Case of Renewable Energy Support Schemes." *Policy Sciences,* 47(3), 267–87. doi:10.1007/s11077–013–9189–7.

Feindt, P. H. and Flynn, A. (2009). "Policy Stretching and Institutional Layering: British Food Policy between Security, Safety, Quality, Health and Climate Change." *British Politics*, 4(3), 386–414. doi:10.1057/bp.2009.13.

Freed, G. L., Andreae, M. C., Cowan, A. E., and Katz, S. L. (2002). "The Process of Public Policy Formulation: The Case of Thimerosal in Vaccines." *Pediatrics*, 109(6), 1153–59.

Gonsalves, J., Becker, T., Braun, A., Campilan, D., De Chavez, H., Fajber, E., Kapiriri, M., Rivaca-Caminade R., and Vernooy, R. (Eds.) (2005). Participatory Research and Development for Sustainable Agriculture and Natural Resource Management: A Sourcebook. International Potato Center—Users' Perspectives with Agricultural Research and Development, Laguna, Philippines and International Development Research Centre, Ottawa, ON, Canada, Volume 3.

Harrington, W. and Morgenstern, R. D. (2004). "Comparing Instrument Choices," in Sterner, T. (Ed.), *Choosing Environmental Policy: Comparing Instruments and Outcomes in the United States and Europe.* Washington DC: RFF Press, pp. 1–22.

Hayes, M. T. (1992). *Incrementalism and Public Policy.* New York: Longmans.

Hendriks, C. M. (October 2009). "Deliberative Governance in the Context of Power." *Policy and Society*, 28(3), 173–84.

Hood, C. (1986). *The Tools of Government.* Chatham: Chatham House Publishers.

Howlett, M. (2009). "Policy Analytical Capacity and Evidence-Based Policy-Making: Lessons from Canada." *Canadian Public Administration*, 52(2), 153–75.

Howlett, M. (2016). "Policy Analytical Capacity," in *Policy and Society*, 34(3–4), 173–82.

Howlett, M. and Cashore, B. (August 2007). "Re-Visiting the New Orthodoxy of Policy Dynamics: The Dependent Variable and Re-Aggregation Problems in the Study of Policy Change." *Canadian Political Science Review*, 1(2), 50–62.

——— (2009). "The Dependent Variable Problem in the Study of Policy Change: Understanding Policy Change as a Methodological Problem." *Journal of Comparative Policy Analysis: Research and Practice*, 11(1), 33–46.

Howlett, M. and Mukherjee, I. (November 2014). "Policy Design and Non-Design: Towards a Spectrum of Policy Formulation Types." *Politics and Governance*, 2(2), 57–71.

Howlett, M. and Ramesh, M. (1993). "Patterns of Policy Instrument Choice: Policy Styles, Policy Learning and the Privatization Experience." *Policy Studies Review*, 12(1), 3–24.

Howlett, M. and Rayner, J. (2013). "Patching vs Packaging in Policy Formulation: Assessing Policy Portfolio Design." *Politics and Governance*, 1(2), 170–82. doi:10.12924/pag2013.01020170.

Howlett, M. and Wellstead, A. (August 2011). "Policy Analysts in the Bureaucracy Revisited: The Nature of Professional Policy Work in Contemporary Government." *Politics & Policy*, 39(4), 613–33.

Howlett, M., Mukherjee, I., and Rayner, J. (June 2014). "The Elements of Effective Program Design: A Two-Level Analysis." *Politics and Governance*, 2(2), 1–12.

Howlett, M., Ramesh, M., and Perl, A. (2009). *Studying Public Policy: Policy Cycles and Policy Subsystems*. Oxford: Oxford University Press.

Hsu, A. (2016). "Measuring Policy Analytical Capacity for the Environment: A Case for Engaging New Actors." *Policy and Society*, 34(3–4), 197–208.

James, T. E. and Jorgensen, P. D. (2009). "Policy Knowledge, Policy Formulation, and Change: Revisiting a Foundational Question." *Policy Studies Journal*, 37(1), 141–62.

Jung, T. and Nutley, S. M. (2008). "Evidence and Policy Networks: The UK Debate about Sex Offender Community Notification." *Evidence & Policy*, 4(2), 187–207.

Justen, A., Schippl, J., Lenz, B., and Fleischer, T. (2013). "Assessment of Policies and Detection of Unintended Effects: Guiding Principles for the Consideration of Methods and Tools in Policy-Packaging." *Transportation Research Part A: Policy and Practice*, 60, 19–30.

Lester, J. P. and Stewart, J. (2000). *Public Policy: An Evolutionary Approach*. Belmont, CA: Wadsworth.

Lindblom, C. E. (1959). "The Science of Muddling Through." *Public Administration Review*, 19(2), 79–88.

Linder, S. H. and Peters, B. G. (1990). "Policy Formulation and the Challenge of Conscious Design." *Evaluation and Program Planning*, 13, 303–11.

Lindquist, E. (2006). "Organizing for Policy Implementation: The Emergence and Role of Implementation Units in Policy Design and Oversight." *Journal of Comparative Policy Analysis: Research and Practice*, 8(4), 311–24.

MacRae, D. and Whittington. D. (1997). *Expert Advice for Policy Choice: Analysis and Discourse*. Washington, DC: Georgetown University Press.

Majone, G. (1975). "On the Notion of Political Feasibility." *European Journal of Political Research*, 3(2), 259–74.

Marier, P. (2008). "Empowering Epistemic Communities: Specialized Politicians, Policy Experts and Policy Reform." *West European Politics*, 31(3), 513–33.

Marier, P. (2009). "The Power of Institutionalized Learning: The Uses and Practices of Commissions to Generate Policy Change." *Journal of European Public Policy*, 16(8), 1204–23.

Massey, E., Biesbroek, R., Huitema, D., and Jordan, A. (November 2014). "Climate Policy Innovation: The Adoption and Diffusion of Adaptation Policies across Europe." *Global Environmental Change*, 29, 434–43. doi:10.1016/j.gloenvcha. 2014.09.002.

Meltsner, A. J. (1972). "Political Feasibility and Policy Analysis." *Public Administration Review*, 32(6), 859–67.

Montpetit, E. (2003). "Public Consultations in Policy Network Environments." *Canadian Public Policy*, 29(1), 95–110.

Mukherjee, I. and Howlett, M.. (August 2015). "Who Is a Stream? Epistemic Communities, Instrument Constituencies and Advocacy Coalitions in Public Policy-Making." *Politics and Governance*, 3(2), 65.

Nair, S. and Howlett, M. (February 2016). "Meaning and Power in the Design and Development of Policy Experiments." *Futures, Policy-making for the long* term: *puzzling and powering to navigate wicked futures issues*, 76, 67–74. doi:10.1016/j.futures.2015.02.008.

Noordegraaf, M. (2000). "Professional Sense-Makers: Managerial Competencies amidst Ambiguities." *International Journal of Public Sector Management*, 13(4), 319–32.

Nutley, S. M., Walter, I., and Davies, H. T. O. (2007). *Using Evidence: How Research Can Inform Public Services*. Bristol: Policy Press.

Öberg, P., Lundin, M., and Thelander, J. (February 2015, 2014). "Political Power and Policy Design: Why Are Policy Alternatives Constrained?" *Policy Studies Journal*, 43(1), 93–114. n/a—n/a. doi:10.1111/psj.12086.

Painter, M. and Pierre, J. (2005). *Challenges to State Policy Capacity: Global Trends and Comparative Perspectives*. London: Palgrave Macmillan.

Pal, L. A. and Clark, I. D. (2016). "Making Reform Stick: Political Acumen as an Element of Political Capacity for Policy Change and Innovation." *Policy and Society*, 2016. doi:10.1016/j.polsoc.2015.09.006.

Pestoff, V. (December 2006). "Citizens and Co-Production of Welfare Services." *Public Management Review*, 8, 503–19. doi:10.1080/14719030601022882.

Pestoff, V. A., Brandsen, T., and Verschuere, B. (2012). *New Public Governance, the Third Sector and Co-Production*. New York: Routledge.

Peters, B. G. (1996). *The Policy Capacity of Government*. Ottawa: Canadian Centre for Management Development.

Pierre, J. (1998). "Public Consultation and Citizen Participation: Dilemmas of Policy Advice," in Peters, B. G. and Savoie, D. J. (Eds.), *Taking Stock: Assessing Public Sector Reforms*. Montreal, QC, Canada: McGill-Queen's Press, pp. 137–63.

Polsby, N. W. (1984). *Political Innovation in America: The Politics of Policy Initiation*. New Haven, CT: Yale University Press.

Prince, M. J. (2007). "Soft Craft, Hard Choices, Altered Context: Reflections on 25 Years of Policy Advice in Canada," in Dobuzinskis, L., Howlett, M., and Laycock, D. (Eds.), *Policy Analysis in Canada: The State of the Art*. Toronto: University of Toronto Press, pp. 95–106.

Putt, A. and Springer, J. (1989). *Policy Research: Concepts, Methods, and Applications*. Upper Saddle River, NJ: Prentice Hall.

Rajagopalan, N. and Rasheed, A. M. A. (1995). "Incremental Models of Policy Formulation and Non-Incremental Changes: Critical Review and Synthesis." *British Journal of Management*, 6,289–302.

Salamon, L. M. (2002). *The Tools of Government: A Guide to the New Governance*. New York: Oxford University Press, 2002.

Schneider, A. and Ingram, H. (1994). "Social Constructions and Policy Design: Implications for Public Administration." *Research in Public Administration*, 3, 137–73.

Sidney, M. S. (2007). "Policy Formulation: Design and Tools," in Fischer, F., Miller, G. J., and Sidney, M. S. (Eds.), *Handbook of Public Policy Analysis: Theory, Politics and Methods*. New Brunswick, NJ: CRC Taylor & Francis, pp. 79–87.

Smith, T. B. (1977). "Advisory Committees in the Public Policy Process." *International Review of Administrative Sciences*, 43(2), 153–66.

Stoker, G., and John, P. (2009). "Design Experiments: Engaging Policy Makers in the Search for Evidence about What Works." *Political Studies*, 57, 336–73.

Stone, D. A. (1988). *Policy Paradox and Political Reason*. Glenview, IL: Scott, Foresman.

Thaler, R. H. and Sunstein, C. R. (2009). *Nudge: Improving Decisions About Health, Wealth, and Happiness. Revised & Expanded Edition*. New York: Penguin Books.

Thelen, K. (2004). *How Institutions Evolve: The Political Economy of Skills in Germany, Britain, the United States and Japan*. Cambridge: Cambridge University Press.

Thomas, H. G. (2001). "Towards a New Higher Education Law in Lithuania: Reflections on the Process of Policy Formulation." *Higher Education Policy*, 14(3), 213–23.

Tiernan, A. (March 2015). "Craft and Capacity in the Public Service." *Australian Journal of Public Administration*, 74(1), 53–62.

United Nations (2007). Common Country Assessment and United Nations Development Assistance Framework. Available online at www.undg.org/docs/6860/2007%20CCA%20and%20UNDAF%20Guidelines%20FINAL.doc.

Van der Heijden, J. (January 2011). "Institutional Layering: A Review of the Use of the Concept." *Politics*, 31(1), 9–18. doi:10.1111/j.1467–9256.2010.01397.x.

Vreugdenhil, H., Taljaard, S., and Slinger, J. H. (2012). "Pilot Projects and Their Diffusion: A Case Study of Integrated Coastal Management in South Africa." *International Journal of Sustainable Development*, 15(1/2), 148. doi:10.1504/IJSD.2012.044039.

Waller, M. (1992). "Evaluating Policy Advice." *Australian Journal of Public Administration*, 51(4), 440–49.

Warwick, P. V. (2000). "Policy Horizons in West European Parliamentary Systems." *European Journal of Political Research*, 38, 37–61.

Weimer, D. and Vining, A. (1992). *Policy Analysis: Concepts and Practice*, Upper Saddle River, NJ: Prentice Hall.

Weimer, D. L. (1993). "The Current State of Design Craft: Borrowing, Tinkering, and Problem Solving." *Public Administration Review*, 53(2), 110–20.

Weir, M.. (1992). "Ideas and the Politics of Bounded Innovation," in Steinmo, S., Thelen, K., and Longstreth, F. (Eds.), *Structuring Politics: Historical Institutionalism in Comparative Analysis*. Cambridge: Cambridge University Press, pp. 188–216.

4 Decision-making

Once a problem has been recognized, taken up for resolution, and alternative solutions to it formulated, then policymakers need to make a decision on what to do. Making such decisions is a more complex task and involves more actors than commonly believed. Many public managers claim to be administrators and, hence, not involved in policy decision-making, which they argue is the function of senior government officials (Svara 2006). This is a misconception, because a large number of policy actors are involved in decision-making: public managers may themselves make decisions which are more policy-related than they think or provide policy recommendations which help shape the decisions of higher-level policymakers (Craft 2015).

The basics of decision-making

What is decision-making?

Decision-making is a task in policy-making involving the selection of a course of action. It involves selecting from among a range of possible policy options, including simply maintaining the status quo. Decisions are not always "positive" in the sense of accomplishing or selecting something new. In many cases decisions are "negative" and involve allowing existing arrangements to stand either unaltered or in only slightly modified form (Howlett 2007). And positive decisions may involve major overhauls of existing arrangements, institutions, rules, and laws or may affect these only at the margins or "incrementally" (Lindblom 1959).

Decision-making in the sense described here occurs in the process of *policy adoption* which follows policy formulation. It is not synonymous with the entire policy-making process, although it is sometimes discussed as if this were so. Decision-making is distinguishable from agenda-setting and policy formulation, for example. Both those tasks involve some decisions, such as deciding to recognize a policy problem or not to pursue particular options in its resolution. However, the kind of decision-making involved in policy selection is different in both the key features of the tasks involved —in this case to make authoritative allocations of resources and time in the pursuit of particular tools and goals, and not others—and also in the narrower range of key players active at this point in the policy process—as these are limited to those with the legal authority to make such allocations, often meaning the legislature and courts as well as administrative bodies. It is also different from policy implementation and evaluation although both those tasks also involve some decision-making activity with respect to, for example, whether or not to pursue violators of regulations for their malfeasance or with respect to what kinds of issues and programs will be evaluated and in what fashion. These decisions remain subordinate to the central decision to go ahead with a particular program or policy which is the essence of the decision-making activity described below.

In general, public policy decision-making consists of:

- the presence of one or more policy proposals that come before authoritative policy actors for selection;
- the presence of a set of decision criteria, however loosely articulated in practice, that decision-makers take with them into the selection process;
- some effort at comparison and ranking of policy proposals, however informally, based on the decision criteria established; and
- a relatively clear determination of a policy option which can be implemented in subsequent phases of policy activity.

This general outline of the decision-making process allows a great deal of variation as to how decisions are made in different countries and sectors and at different times. Decision-making processes vary according to the nature of the decision-makers involved, the source and content of their authority to make binding decisions and the institutional contexts in which they deliberate.

Different countries have different constitutional and organizational arrangements and operating procedures, all of which have a significant impact on the decision-making processes they follow and in which policy actors and managers must have expertise. In addition, decision-making processes are also influenced by who the decision-makers themselves are. These individuals vary tremendously in background, knowledge, and values, and this in turn affects how they approach their tasks and the factors they consider in making their decisions. While it is true that most judges and legislators in most countries are lawyers (and hence one might expect some familiarity and respect for the rule and practices of law), many other professions and orientations are also found in the upper and lower houses of parliaments and congresses in which many public policy decisions are made. And civil services employ a diverse array of experts tasked with making authoritative decisions on their behalf.

As a result of these contextual factors, decision-makers in different settings respond differently when dealing with similar problems, and as any observer of parliamentary and legislative behavior knows all too well, it is difficult to predict exactly what kinds of decision will emerge from their deliberations and votes. However, many decision-making bodies, such as regulatory agencies and the courts, also share some common motivations and patterns of policy-making behavior, and are commonly bound by legislation and judicial precedents. These provide some structure and continuity, and an element of predictability, to many public policy choices and selections. It is equally true, however, that in many country contexts—and probably in all countries at certain points—decision-making suffers from the lack of an institutionalized or transparent process, or is beset by corruption and conflicts-of-interest, making the attempt to introduce systematic, evidence-based inputs to decision-making, or to make predictions with respect to decision-making outcomes, extremely problematic.

Actors in decision-making

It is a common perception that decision-making is the more or less exclusive business of senior administrators and elected officials, and is therefore dominated by political rather than administrative or technical considerations. Decision-making is indeed highly political because policy decisions often create winners or losers, whose real and anticipated reactions to the different policy options play an essential role in shaping policy decisions. However, it is a misperception that policy decisions are driven exclusively by political considerations. Other considerations, such as the potential effectiveness of policies in achieving intended policy goals and their impacts on the society over the long run, demand technical expertise and professional analysis. Decision-making is thus often more technical, and less political, than often assumed.

While it is true that elite members of governments are the main players in formal decision-making, public policies may take many forms, and other policy actors within the government can be involved in decision-making in various capacities. First of all, public policy decisions can be acts, laws, regulatory guidance, and/or procedural measures, many of which may be decided at different levels of government agencies so that the final elite "decision" is merely to approve a kind of patchwork of previous, subordinate choices made by public managers. This is especially the case where the policy issues or solutions are highly technical. The top-level approval in such cases is often more a procedural requirement than substantive in nature.

Second, even for the policies for which substantial input from top executives and legislative bodies is sought, the policy options reaching these decision-makers may reflect the preferences and alternatives developed by public managers at various levels within the government. Third, even when they do not propose specific alternatives, public managers are often asked by high-level policymakers to prepare policy analysis of their preferred policy options, or to provide technical information and professional advice on various aspects of those options, such as their potential effectiveness and administrative feasibility. This again allows public managers to have a significant impact on final decisions that flow from these deliberations and choice opportunities.

There are also other actors involved in decision-making, such as professional analysts, issue-specific experts, consultants, and lobbyists, although their participation can best be categorized as indirect since their influence on policy adoption is felt indirectly through their affiliations or associations with decision-makers. For example, professional analysts in the Congressional Budgetary Office (CBO) in the US are regularly involved in providing policy analysis on key policy decisions facing legislators. And in some relatively rare instances the public itself can also be directly involved in decision-making when public referendums are used. In 1959, for example, a Swiss national referendum rejected a proposal to give women the right to vote, thus delaying universal suffrage in the country by another 32 years.

Ultimately, organizational aspects of policy and administration are critical in decision-making, because in the end policies are carried out or supervised by specific government agencies. The capacities of these agencies in policy implementation and adaptation play an essential role in shaping policy decisions through their impact on the considerations and perceptions of the feasibility of policy choices.

This tripod of political, technical, and organizational considerations is a distinct feature of public policy decision-making, compared to decision-making in the private sector which is usually more focused on profit-making criteria. The decision-makers' ability to integrate these three aspects in their choices often determines the quality of public decisions and eventually policy effectiveness.

Decision-making models

Policy scientists use a variety of models to capture the dynamics of public policy decision-making. They categorize decision-making into three main types depending on the extent to which information is known about likely policy outcomes.

The first model is the "rational" decision model which attributes primacy to logical reasoning and evidence. Following instrumental thinking, the model proposes decision-makers should choose the option that maximizes the attainment of their individual goals and values (see Meyerson and Banfield 1955; Simon 1983). The model is "rational" in the sense that it can—at least in theory—lead to the most efficient possible means of achieving policy goals. Although the rational decision model is appealing due to its commitment to getting the job done, questions are raised about its neglect of ethics and democratic processes (DeLeon and Longobardi 2002; Garrison 2000; Richardson 2002).

And critics also raise concerns about its practicality. The applicability of the model is hampered by the need for a large amount of accurate information on policy impacts and consequences of many possible policy alternatives—information that may be impractical or impossible to obtain in the usually short timeframe in which decision-makers must act. It also assumes a uniformity of purpose and framing of problems among decision-makers which may be lacking. Failing this unity, there will likely be no agreement on the basic criteria against which to assess a particular policy option. And decisions may be shared among many actors—many or all of whom are unwilling or unable to dispassionately weigh the aggregate costs and benefits of a particular decision. In such cases, the outcomes of a "rational" process are likely to be less optimal and efficient than expected or advertised.

The limitations of the rational decision model, despite its seeming common-sense appeal, have led to a search for more holistic and normative policy theory (DeLeon and Longobardi 2002; John 1998; Parsons 1995; Sabatier 1999). Two of the better-known models used to understand decision-making in the real world include "incremental" and "garbage can" models.

The "incremental" decision model analyzes public decision-making as a time- and information-constrained process characterized by conflict, bargaining, and compromise among self-interested decision-makers. Rather than adopt "maximizing" alternatives, in this model it is expected that decisions arrived at through bargaining will be the result of the "successive limited comparisons" decision-makers make of new proposals against the results of earlier decisions, resulting typically in only "marginal" or "incremental" changes from the previous *status quo*. In this model, the decisions eventually made represent more what is politically feasible in the sense of satisfying the interests of various participants rather than what might be technically desirable in a more certain policy climate.

According to Lindblom (1959), there are two major reasons why policy decisions typically do not stray far away from the *status quo*. First, since the status quo already represents an interest-based compromise, it is politically more feasible to continue the existing pattern of distribution of goods and services than to alter the system dramatically through the redistribution typically required of any radically new proposals. Second, the standard operating procedures and administrative practices of bureaucracies charged with implementing existing policies also tend to favor minor modifications of existing practices over major overhaul.

The second alternative to rational decision models is the so-called "garbage can" model which applies when there is a very large number of decision-makers and a great deal of uncertainty about both the causes of problems and their solution. In such situations, policy outcomes will lack a great deal of rationality and will instead reflect the temporary desires of those actually able to dominate, however transitorily, the decision-making process. In this model, the idea of maximization found in the rational model, or the "optimization" found in the incremental model, is largely abandoned. Instead it is argued that a "satisficing" principle is likely to emerge in which decision-making involves simply satisfying whatever standards or goals have been set by this group of policymakers at the time of decision. According to this model, the search for a policy response to a policy problem will end when a policy option at hand is perceived to be able to produce "acceptable" results as defined by the standards set by influential decision-makers. As a result, the full range of policy alternatives with potentially better results is never fully explored. Decision-makers thus would look beyond a relatively small range of policy options at hand only if these options fail to produce a satisfactory or satisficing outcome.

The decision-making process

Choosing a policy scheme that can address a problem and lead towards preferred outcomes requires a great deal of forethought in assessing which policy option will be most appropriate (Weimer and Vining 2011: 354).

Analysis for decision-making

Decision processes often involve technical analysis, and are oriented in many cases towards economic measurements and assessments with the aim of identifying a "maximizing" choice, one which maximizes effectiveness and, especially, efficiency. This can involve the use of standardized decision-aid techniques—such as multi-goal or multi-criteria analysis, formal cost-benefit analysis, qualitative cost-benefit analysis, or cost-effectiveness analysis—in order to help identify "optimal" or "maximizing" choices.

The choice of technique employed by managers often depends on whether (economic) efficiency is the only concern of a policy or if other concerns are also present. Furthermore, different types of analysis will become possible depending on whether or not efficiency impacts are quantifiable and/or other goals can be monetized and therefore readily compared. (Boardman et al. 2001). The complexity in choosing a maximizing policy increases with both the number of goals and the difficulties involved in quantifying them (Weimer and Vining 2011: 353). In the most complex situations, decision-makers face difficult trade-offs and may not be able to settle on a "maximizing" outcome, but rather must opt for a "satisfycing" one (Bendor et al. 2009).

In *formal cost-benefit analysis*, analysis proceeds along relatively simple lines. In this case, efficiency is set out as the dominant criterion, and the analysis revolves around determining which option yields the best value (think of a manager choosing between two equal goods offered at different prices). Of course, in many cases the choice in policy will be more complex, with various, sometimes contradictory, goals being sought at the same time. The key here is that all goals must be amenable to monetization so that their benefits and costs can be readily compared. Through this type of analysis, decision-makers can assess how alternatives should be ranked in against each other, and which among them should be selected (Weimer and Vining 2011: 358). A *qualitative cost-benefit analysis* is used when not all of the efficiency impacts can be expressed in monetary units. This may be the case when environmental or cultural policies are in play, for example. A policy analyst conducting such an assessment may be hard-pressed to correctly monetize the loss of a pristine wetland or of a literary festival.

It is also very common for policy areas to involve more than just an efficiency goal. Analysts may wish to separate those elements of a policy option having impacts that can be monetized from those that cannot. When this happens, "multi-goal analysis" (Weimer and Vining 2011: 357) is useed. If efficiency is flanked by just one other goal and the policy manager can monetize both goals, *modified cost-benefit analysis* may still be employed.

However, if the additional goals can be quantified but not monetized, then *cost-effectiveness analysis* is an approach often used to clarify the strengths and weaknesses of decision alternatives. Here analysts use a fixed budget method whereby a certain amount of money is chosen to be spent and then the policy option that provides the most benefits is selected without necessarily calculating costs. As an alternative, fixed effectiveness approaches set the level of benefits to be reached and then the policy option that provides that level at the lowest cost is chosen. Not all goals can be quantified or monetized, leading to the employment of both quantitative and qualitative measures (Vining and Boardman 2007: 76).

The assessment of various options provides opportunities for policy innovation, as information revealed through a comparison of different options can aid policy design by prompting the reformulation of certain options and the identification of mitigation strategies for others. Various components in different options can be reconfigured into new combinations that might then lead to win-win options, and mitigation strategies can be developed to reduce particular negative impacts for options that are preferable along other dimensions. Too much attention is often devoted to the trade-offs between different objectives, while innovative opportunities for synergy are overlooked.

Nevertheless, in most cases, some alternatives will score highest on certain criteria and others on other criteria, necessitating implicit or explicit trade-offs to be made in the decision-making process. Before value judgments are made on which trade-offs are worth making, it is critical to identify them, and the use of techniques such as decision matrices can facilitate the process (see Box 4.1).

Policy analysis, regardless of how comprehensive it appears, however, is but one input for decision-makers. A final decision not to adopt *any* policy option—even the best ranked one along all dimensions—is always possible as well. Political imperatives, narrowly defined agency interests, and decision-makers' self-interests are also important considerations for decision-makers and the final decision is often an outcome of strategic interaction and compromise among multiple decision-makers.

Reports and recommendations from policy managers at the highest levels —such as cabinet secretaries and clerks—must ensure that decision points that are inherently complex are accurately and appropriately summarized, in a concise fashion. They must guard against a number of potential biases that can affect decision-making, such as:

- groupthink—a process in which group pressures for conformity undermine systematic consideration of alternatives and disconfirming evidence;
- a bias toward criteria for which quantitative measures are available;
- a bias toward positive impacts; and
- a bias toward the study of impacts along a particular dimension that is closely associated with the identity of the organizations conducting the assessment (such as environmental impacts for an environmental NGO).

Box 4.1 Decision matrix

A convenient way to systematically organize information required for effective decision-making is to display it in the form of a decision matrix, which typically will display policy choices across the columns and decision criteria down the rows. Any cell in the decision matrix contains the projected outcome of the alternative assessed with reference to the column criterion. For example, Cell A1 contains information on the outcome of Alternative A as assessed with reference to Criterion 1.

To aid the decision-making process, each alternative in the matrix should be linked to each criterion systematically. To protect against or counter some potential biases of the analyst, all cells should be considered, which promotes recognition and discussion of oversights and biases.

Criteria	Alternative A	Alternative B	Alternative C	Alternative . . .
Criterion 1	A1	B1	C1	. . .
Criterion 2	A2	B2	C2	. . .
Criterion 3	A3	B3	C3	. . .
Criterion . . .				. . .

Source: D. MacRae and D. Whittington (1997) *Expert Advice for Policy Choice: Analysis and Discourse.* Washington, DC: Georgetown University Press

Things can get decidedly more complicated for decision-making when trade-offs between different dimensions of a problem are necessary. However, clearly communicating one's technical analysis remains of great value in contributing to a sound decision, not least because it forces the decision-makers to openly share their values with other actors. In a democratic context, for example, the other actors might often include the general public, which can benefit from the provision of good information about various policy options. Such information can help different stakeholders to participate at a higher level and have a greater impact in the decision-making process, giving the process a better chance of moving towards optimality.

Policy selection

As set out above, decision-making in the public policy world is about "policy selection," or choosing and officially sanctioning one or more of the alternatives developed in policy formulation. This is a process that can involve one or multiple decision-makers, understood to be those individuals and actors imbued with authority to make such selections.

Of course, governments are complex structures, and public policy decisions may be made at the local or district, regional or county, provincial or state, and national or international levels. Exactly which actor is empowered to make an authoritative selection in which jurisdiction is typically set out in constitutional documents, albeit often in vague and general terms. Sorting out these jurisdictional issues is often one of the main functions of the judiciary, which itself is organized hierarchically, from local small claims courts to state and provincial supreme courts. The final say in many cases rests with key national bodies such as national parliaments, legislatures and congresses, and supreme courts, although some supra-national bodies also exercise some of these functions, as occurs in world trade tribunals and bodies of the United Nations, the European and African Unions, and other such multilateral and bilateral bodies (Kahler 1989). Thus, decision-makers may include:

- members of bureaucracies acting in accordance with legal rights and authority granted to them by legislatures and political executives;
- those same legislatures and executives issuing legal acts and executive orders and rules; or
- members of the judiciary who can overturn such rules and orders, and sometimes replace them with their own rulings, in the name of constitutional mandates and conventions.

In making their selections and decisions, these actors operate in very different venues, with different resources and purposes and very different attitudes towards criteria such as fairness and evidence. In the bureaucracy, for example, considerations of the feasibility of implementing a decision and concerns about legality and mandates are often highlighted. Administrative decisions must be made in accordance with legal mandates in order to be upheld by political executives and the courts. They are also commonly made in the name of criteria such as budgetary efficiency and likely outcome effectiveness, often on the basis of experience and evidence gathered over many years by senior civil servants about "what works" in dealing with a problem (Breyer et al. 1998).

In the judiciary, other criteria are typically highlighted. Selections are typically made by legal experts (judges) based on past precedents, on their interpretations of the constitutional and legal rights of both those making decisions and those affected by them, and on their assessment of the facts and evidence used by other decision-makers to support their decisions (Bricker 2015).

In the political branches of government, on the other hand, selections may be made for completely different reasons, with little respect for legal niceties or past precedents. Decisions may be based on factors such as political, electoral, or legislative expediency in the process of cobbling together majority support among lawmakers for any particular choice; and in this process, considerations of feasibility may take a back seat to symbolic politics or the political need to deliver government largesse to the clients and supporters of various parties, factions, or individual members of the legislature. Some systems of government that accentuate the need to form and preserve political coalitions, along with others that empower individual members of the legislature, indirectly incentivize such behavior, while other systems that promote stable party majorities tend to do the opposite (Warwick 2006). However, even those parliamentary systems that place the legislature under the control of the executive are not immune from clientelistic and electoral activity (Goetz 2007).

Members of political executives—cabinet ministers, prime ministers and their staff—play a major role in public policy decision-making. Like the judiciary, these involve relatively small numbers of individuals, although the number expands dramatically if one includes mayors and councilors at the local level. These executives are typically quite experienced, having taken some time to rise to their positions through party and legislative ranks. Their educational backgrounds vary greatly, however, meaning their familiarity with specific issues also is uncertain and fluctuates with different appointments. Nevertheless, there is usually some effort made to link expertise to the appointment or election of ministers, although other criteria such as gender, ethnic group status, or regional representation are also commonly used in cabinet level appointments. The nature of the relationships between ministers and prime ministers or presidents is also variable, with some relationships being clearly hierarchical—with prime ministers or presidents in charge—while in others they are more equal; and such relationships may also change over time (Bernier et al. 2005). Furthermore, the extent to which a country is de-centralized, or exists as a federation or confederal unit, also leads to variations in both the number of cabinet positions and the nature of their relationship to each other and to public policy decision-making. In some highly de-centralized federations, such as Canada or Switzerland, for example, subnational executives may individually or collectively hold as much power and authority as nominally "national" ones (Radin and Boase 2000).

There is also the issue of the *timing* of decisions. In some cases, decisions may be made quickly, as might for example occur when a country is invaded and its legislature declares war; or decisions can take many years to emerge. The archetype of a public policy decision is a clear-cut ruling by a court (for example, to overturn legislation) or the passage of a bill into law by a legislature. But in many situations, especially in the bureaucracy, it is much more difficult to pin down and identify when exactly a selection has been made, who made it, and why (Weiss 1980). Discussions and proposals for selections can flow up and down through the administration for many years, resulting in a process of "decision accretion" as rounds of decision-making activity result in final decisions emerging in layers from this process (Teisman 2000). This can make tracing the origins and reasons for one selection being made rather than another hard to discern.

It also is not necessarily the case that a decision will be taken when it is needed. In legislatures, for example, bargaining between parties and factions can tie up legislation for months if not years. Similarly, the process of decision-making in bureaucracies can also be drawn out, as is also the case in the judiciary when decisions are taken in lower courts and then appealed to higher levels, with each step involving prolonged argumentation. The torturous journey of the American Health Care Act (popularly known as Obamacare) is an extreme example of lengthy decision-making processes, especially in presidential systems of government.

Challenges in decision-making

In a perfect world, decisions would be taken in a timely manner, take into account all relevant available information, and do so in a fair and unbiased way with an eye towards achieving the best possible outcomes over the medium to long term. Unfortunately, however, as anyone who reads the newspapers and pays attention to government practices and policy outcomes knows, this scenario occurs all too rarely. Instead, many decisions are taken at the wrong time, examine or respond only to very partial and less than impartial information, and do so with a focus on very short-term outcomes and narrow benefits, including personal enrichment of corrupt officials or the promotion of electoral or career advantages of politicians in the next election and civil servants or cabinet officials in the next ministerial shuffle or budget process.

Why does this happen? Is there anything that can be done to move from the latter scenario to the former? In some cases it is very difficult to avoid problems which lead to sub-optimal or very poor decisions. Decision-makers often face:

Short time horizons. As we have seen, the time horizon facing decision-makers is often too short to adequately assess the various effects of policy proposals, especially those that deviate significantly from current policies and practices. This can be the result of a crisis—which by definition implies limited time availability and the need to act quickly. It could also arise from poor administrative planning and/or political foresight. As a result, long-term benefits and costs may be hard to identify, or given much less weight than short-term and more immediately obvious ones.

Lack of reliable information. Much high-quality information is needed to adequately assess policy options in sometimes highly uncertain future scenarios. Such information may simply be unavailable, available only at a very high cost or require a level of analytical sophistication that many decision-makers and analysts don't have; these problems may be particularly pronounced in developing country settings.

Lack of expertise in policy analysis. The analysis of policy proposals can be highly complex, but very few administrative officials, and even fewer elected or appointed politicians, possess the necessary training and experience to carry out proper analysis. The situation is further compounded in many developing countries where remuneration for civil servants is relatively low compared to the private sector, and thus government agencies often lose out to the private sector in competition to recruit or retain the few professional analysts available with adequate training and skills to carry out the kinds of analyses cited above.

While these are serious problems and it may be next to impossible to change these conditions (such as the short-lead time often linked to emergencies), the impact of these constraints under which decision-makers operate should not be exaggerated. Politicians in democratic societies need to be re-elected, of course, and the views of voters about their policy positions and competences cannot be ignored. But governments in many contexts also manage to deal with issues such as environmental protection, forest replanting, and provision of pension plans, which by definition are very long term and transcend short-term electoral considerations (Jacobs 2008). Similarly, while much evidence shows that the results of academic studies and expert advice are often ignored by government, there are also many examples where expert consultations and the examination of research results have played a significant role in policy-making (Nutley 2007). And while some decisions are delayed so long that they emerge well after they are needed, others do occur in a timely fashion and are able to deal effectively with issues ranging from epidemics to earthquakes ('t Hart et al. 2001).

What do these examples of strong decision-making have in common? One is strong leadership together with an organizational culture and set of routines that supports and facilitates high-quality, evidence-based decision-making (Head et al. 2014). It is critically important that political leaders do not panic and rush into judgment and action, or pander to special interests and short-term considerations. Rather, they should act prudently based on best available evidence. While the ability of governments to engage in such analyses is sometimes constrained by a lack of information or resources

(Howlett 2009), such activity is also very much an expression of leadership and decision-maker styles and priorities (Tummers and Kries 2016).

Poor outcomes often result from policy decisions made quickly, often by small groups of isolated decision-makers, without careful attention to their practicality, leading to large gaps between policy design and implementation. In the Philippines, for example, a decision to decentralize key social services such as health and education from central to local government was made without due attention being paid to the lack of planning capacity at the local level (Araral 2006). Bureaucrats with the necessary experience and skills in planning are often reluctant to be reallocated from capital cities, and without them, decision-making in the regions can flounder. Effective issue management and institutional and process design, coupled with forward thinking and anticipatory preparation in terms of information and human resource development, is required to offset such conditions.

Another key factor is the ability and willingness of leaders and other decision-makers to learn (Bennett and Howlett 1992) and their ability to make mistakes without suffering significant damage to their reputations and electoral and career fortunes. Viewed this way, all policy actions are real-time, real-life experiments, in that the circumstances and environment, and the actors and players involved in a decision, are in constant flux. Even with the best intentions, the replication of decisions made in other jurisdictions or sectors will often fail to produce the same results. Being able to reassess and adjust a decision once it has been made is critical if learning is to take place (Gleeson et al. 2015). Some political systems provide enough accountability and autonomy to decision-makers to allow this to happen; others are less forgiving, resulting in a failure to draw appropriate lessons from policy success or failure (Dunlop 2009). Governments and their opposition alike should not be too ready to attribute blame and claim credit for their actions (Hood 2007), but should realize that determining the reasons why policies succeed and fail takes time, and adjust their electoral and other accountability and performance measures accordingly.

Strategies for effective decision-making

Being prepared to deal with surprises is a critical component of successful decision-making (Nair and Howlett 2017). Policy decisions, even on technical issues, are often dominated by immediate imperatives and made without careful consideration of their broader, longer-term implications. During the 1997–98 Asian financial crisis, for example, a series of ad hoc decisions by the Suharto government in Indonesia contributed to the worsening of the economy and eventually led to its own collapse.

Policy decisions can also be hijacked by ideological obsessions or even by the fantasies of political leaders. The Great Leap Forward in China in the 1950s, which was responsible for millions of deaths from famine and other causes, was largely motivated by the unrealistic aspirations of Mao Zedong, China's leader at the time.

More recently, the ideological conviction on the part of policymakers in several developing countries (and of the multilateral institutions that advised and/or pressured them) that the adoption of market principles could improve policy outcomes and efficiency in many sectors also led to an ill-considered rush to privatize and deregulate many industries and social services. As a result, many of these moves were subsequently followed by re-nationalization and re-regulation of many of these activities (Pritchett and Woolcock 2004).

As noted above, these kinds of poor decisions are more likely to occur when policy decisions are controlled and manipulated by a small number of political executives or policy advisors whose personal interests are closely associated with the decisions. These groups' personal and institutional biases can have a detrimental impact on the quality of their decisions and, subsequently, on policy outcomes. This is the case with many military, police, and authoritarian regimes—as in the Great Leap Forward example cited above—but it can also happen in more pluralistic states. For example, the domination of decision-making processes by the small groups of national security advisors surrounding US President George W. Bush and UK Prime Minister Tony Blair led to ill-informed decisions to invade Iraq in 2003, despite these leaders having access to analytical capacities rivalling those of any government in the world (Steele 2016).

A similar situation can result when policy decisions made by one agency are inconsistent and even in conflict with policies implemented by other agencies. This lack of "horizontality" and coordination, for example, is apparent in many countries in areas such as sustainable development and environmental protection, which require a great deal of intra- and inter-governmental coordination—something that is often lacking. This can result in situations, for example, where employment incentives are offered to industries to locate in regions that are environmentally sensitive, under-mining undergoing enhanced protection from parks and wilderness agencies.

The bottom line in all these cases is that in the absence of a logical and orderly process of assessing proposed options against likely future scenarios, decisions are often made in an haphazard manner. This is true even when adequate information and time are available and the decision-making context would in theory allow a closer approximation to a "maximizing" model. Poor policy planning in non-crisis situations can also lead to poor results, as when, for example, decision-makers run up against electoral or parliamentary timetables and are forced to curtail their policy deliberations and adopt ill-considered or "quick" decisions (Bovens and t'Hart 2016).

Some strategies are available to decision-makers and policy managers that might help them to avoid these kinds of error-prone, sub-optimal decisions.

Integrating political, technical, and organizational considerations

A common shortcoming in real-world decision-making is that important considerations beyond the immediate policy goals are often neglected. Decision criteria guide decision-making by providing standards against which policy consequences can be judged as being important or valuable, and help identify less obvious aspects and ramifications of policy choices. Missing a critical criterion may lead to poor decisions—as the consequences that would have been measured by the missing criterion could potentially have shifted the calculation of the costs and benefits.

Decision criteria differ from policy objectives, which are often expressed in a single dimension and in vague terms such as "cutting pollution by 50 percent" or "increasing access to safe drinking water for the poor." These criteria are used to measure the practicality of various options, and the use of the same criteria across different policy options ensures that alternatives can be compared systematically. More explicit and specific definitions of criteria can help to clarify assessments by proposing standards that are measurable and help policymakers focus attention towards the interlinkages among policy objectives across different policy sectors.

This latter feature of decision criteria is critical for the pursuit of sustainable development, for example, which requires the joint consideration of multiple objectives across time and sectors. When compared to economic outcomes, it takes a long time for environmental and social impacts to manifest themselves, and thus less attention is often paid to these aspects of a decision. Consider, for instance, the effects of failing to calculate the cost of storing radioactive waste for 100,000 years in costing a new nuclear reactor.

Criteria need to be selected and formulated strategically so that they represent important concerns to decision-makers and the public. For example, merely reporting pollution levels may not capture decision-makers' and the public's imaginations. These actors may not appreciate the severity of an environmental problem unless the levels are related to how they could affect daily life. Therefore, using health threats as criteria may be more effective in communicating the importance of environmental impacts than presenting environmental impacts in terms of pollution levels.

Mandating and requiring decision-makers to jointly consider key objectives in a multi-criteria policy is another strategy that can also help balance the inclinations of governmental agencies to emphasize only those goals or objectives with which they are most closely associated. Imposing mandatory requirements to consider items such as the impacts on federal-state relations, or on gender equity, can help ensure that multiple key objectives are considered in all policy decisions. Because of the difficulties involved in such analyses, organizations have little incentive to develop such resources unless they are mandated or "mainstreamed." Imposing such requirements helps strengthen public managers' arguments for the need for capacity-building in their agency in order to properly assess impacts which their organizations may not be accustomed to evaluate (Hankivsky 2013). Such requirements can also help organizations to develop policy options and evidence that highlight synergies among otherwise seemingly conflicting objectives and can help expand the horizons of organizations in search of innovative solutions.

Basing decisions on systematic analysis

Establishing a baseline is the first critical step toward more systematic analysis, but it is one which is often neglected in policy practice. A "baseline" here means an accurate assessment of the "business-as-usual" scenario, or what would happen if there were no change in government decisions and existing trends simply continued. This provides a necessary starting point for assessments of the effects of proposed and actual policy interventions. Without the baseline, the option of "let present trends continue" is typically dropped out of consideration, leaving the door open for policy interventions that might aggravate policy problems rather than improve them. Sometimes poorly designed policies are worse than no policy at all.

Note that this baseline is different from the status quo, because it can accommodate changes arising from a range of sources, including the effects of other policies in existence. The time span for a baseline assessment should be the same as the time horizon used to assess policy options. Because a baseline requires extrapolation of current trends and calculation of their effects, collecting the information necessary for establishing a policy baseline is technically challenging and time-consuming. The following information is required to establish such a baseline:

- current conditions (or status quo);
- current and expected trends;
- effects of policies already being implemented; and
- effects of other foreseeable policies or programs.

Box 4.2: Contesting imagined futures of the Affordable Care Act

In March 2017 the Republican-controlled legislative and executive branches in the US attempted to "repeal and replace" the Affordable Care Act, and the House of Representatives was considering a bill that would do exactly that. As for all such major pieces of legislation, the non-partisan Congressional Budget Office (CBO) developed a "scoring" of the costs and benefits of the proposed legislation, one that estimated that under the new legislation, up to 25 million fewer individuals would be covered by health insurance after a 10-year period. The CBO was then fiercely attacked by the new bill's proponents, who claimed that the estimates were greatly exaggerated, since the CBO had failed (according to these critics) to incorporate a baseline in which the ACA insurance markets would completely collapse in a "let present trends continue" scenario. This example shows both the importance of baseline numbers to the assessment of policy options, and the politicization of even supposedly neutral policy analysis in the United States at present.

Source: see www.usatoday.com/story/news/politics/2017/03/15/fact-check-both-parties-spin-cbo-report-republican-health-care-bill/99203010/

While assembling this information may be costly (and contested—see Box 4.2), astute managers will do so well in advance of need, when collecting and analyzing large amounts of data may be difficult or impossible given time constraints.

Assessing economic, social, and environmental impacts of policy options

Decision-making is typically confronted with various uncertainties because information to support accurate predictions of the outcome of policy choices is often inadequate. But there are different types of uncertainty depending on whether they are related to knowledge of the policy problem and its trends, to the impact of policy solutions, or to the policy process and its outcomes. Some can be handled with statistical methods, while others can be reduced through further research. However, some uncertainties are inherent and cannot be reduced. For example, predictions with regard to global warming are inherently uncertain and cast a constant shadow over policy debate on climate change.

Decision-makers must deal with this uncertainty. To help them do so, policy analysts can project the likely outcomes of different policy options against each individual criterion in order to provide decision-makers with "best guess" estimates of risks and outcomes. Such a task is the most challenging, and technical, part of the decision-making process, since it involves the inherent and irreducible uncertainty of projections, despite the availability of various tools and techniques to try to take this uncertainty into account (Walker et al. 2013).

Such assessments may take place as part of the policy formulation process, but may also be carried out (again) in decision-making. The aim is to provide policymakers with solid empirical information—data or evidence-derived—about the likely direction, magnitude, duration, and reversibility of economic, social, and environmental changes resulting from the policy options under consideration.

Strengthen analytical capacity

The importance of the careful analysis of policy options doesn't imply that all public managers themselves must be experts in all of the techniques and applications of policy analysis. But they can play an instrumental role in fostering the development of policy analysis capacity both within and outside government. They can take advantage of the world-wide growth in the number of public policy programs and schools by recruiting professional analysts with proper training in policy analysis, and they can also send their staff to short training courses to strengthen their analytical capacity. It is also important to provide institutional support for professional analysts, such as the creation of dedicated department units, or "policy shops," focusing on policy analysis and planning, as well as ensuring there are adequate resources for them to carry out their work. In these ways, policy analysis becomes an attractive career path for talented new recruits.

Governments can contribute to the development of policy analytical capacity outside government. Using new information technologies to tap into expertise that is distributed throughout society is a powerful tool that can drive innovation and quality improvement and can be harnessed to improved decision-making (Noveck 2016). Promoting the participation of (and in some cases competition between) a broader range of actors in internal and external policy assessments can often save costs, improving both the data and the techniques available to decision-makers, and can help to bridge knowledge gaps that exist in the understanding of key policy issues. Since they are less likely to be constrained by the sorts of political and institutional constraints facing government agencies, such inclusion may also help to reduce the risk of having assessments hijacked by narrowly defined organizational and personal interests. All this is predicated on governments being willing to mandate more transparency and share information with other governmental and nongovernmental agencies.

Improving intra-agency and interagency linkage in decision-making

Many contemporary policy problems are multidimensional in nature, crossing jurisdictional and other boundaries established in previous eras. This is especially true of vertically "siloed" government agencies that are structured to pursue specific notions of the origins and solutions of policy problems. Public managers can promote "horizontality" through the creation of international, intergovernmental, or interagency bodies that can help to broaden the type of considerations incorporated into policy analysis. Enhanced conversations, consultations, and cooperation with other members of the policy community within and outside the government can be expected to lead to improved decision-making.

Conclusion: better decisions help improve implementation and outcomes

Policy decisions cap the "front-end" process of policy-making, which begins with agenda-setting and proceeds to formulation. The decision-making stage of the policy process is more political than the preceding processes, in that it is handled by more senior appointed and elected officials; but it is also more technical. In addition to astute political judgment, the success of decision-making depends on evidence and sound analysis, something that public managers are often best placed to offer. They need to rise to this challenge if public policies are not to falter at the "back-end" stage of policy implementation, the subject of the following chapter.

References

Araral, E. K. (2006). "The Political Economy of Policy Reform in the Philippines: 1992–1998." *Journal of Policy Reform*, 9(4), 261–74.

Bardach, E. (2000). *A Practical Guide for Policy Analysis: The Eightfold Path to more Effective Problem Solving*. New York: Chatham House Publishers.

Bendor, J., Sunil, K., and David, S. A. (2009). "Satisficing: A 'Pretty Good' Heuristic." *The B.E. Journal of Theoretical Economics*, 9(1). doi:10.2202/1935–1704.1478.

Bennett, C. J. and Howlett, M. (1992). "The Lessons of Learning: Reconciling Theories of Policy Learning and Policy Change." *Policy Sciences*, 25(3), 275–94.

Bernier, L., Brownsey, K., and Howlett, M. (Eds.) (2005). *Executive Styles in Canada: Cabinet Structures and Leadership Practices in Canadian Government. 1st edn.* Toronto: University of Toronto Press.

Boardman, A. E., Greenberg, D. H., Vining, R., and Weimer, D. L. (2001). *Cost-Benefit Analysis: Concepts and Practice.* Upper Saddle River, NJ: Prentice Hall.

Bovens, M. and t'Hart, P. (May 2016). "Revisiting the Study of Policy Failures." *Journal of European Public Policy,* 23(5), 653–66. doi:10.1080/13501763. 2015.1127273.

Braybrooke, D. and Lindblom, C. (1963). *A Strategy of Decision: Policy Evaluation as a Social Process.* New York: Free Press of Glencoe.

Breyer, S. G., Stewart, R. B., Sunstein, C. R., and Spitzer, M. L. (1998). *Administrative Law and Regulatory Policy: Problems, Text, and Cases. 4th edn.* Aspen Law & Business.

Bricker, B. (2015). *Visions of Judicial Review: A Comparative Examination of Courts and Policy in Democracies. 1st edition.* S.l.: ECPR Press.

Cohen, M., March, J., and Olsen, J. (1972). "A Garbage Can Model of Organizational Choice." *Administrative Science Quarterly,* 17(1), 1–25.

Craft, J. (January 2015). "Revisiting the Gospel: Appointed Political Staffs and Core Executive Policy Coordination." *International Journal of Public Administration,* 38(1), 56–65. doi:10.1080/01900692.2014.928316.

DeLeon, P. and Longobardi, R. C. (2002). "Policy Analysis in the Good Society." *The Good Society,* 11(1), 37–41.

Dunlop, C. A. (2009). "Policy Transfer as Learning: Capturing Variation in What Decision-Makers Learn from Epistemic Communities." *Policy Studies,* 30(3), 289–311.

Garrison, J. (2000). "Pragmatism and Public Administration." *Administration & Society,* 32(4), 458–77.

Gleeson, D., Dwyer, J., Lin, V., Legge, D,, and Hughes, A. (November 2015). "Can Learning Sets Help Policy Managers with Their Wicked Problems?" *Health Services Management Research,* 951484815616828. doi:10.1177/ 0951484815616828.

Goetz, A. M. (2007). "Manoeuvring Past Clientelism: Institutions and Incentives to Generate Constituencies in Support of Governance Reforms." *Commonwealth and Comparative Politics,* 45(4), 403–24.

Hankivsky, O. (2013). "Gender Mainstreaming: A Five-Country Examination." *Politics & Policy,* 41(5), 629–655. doi:10.1111/polp.12037.

Head, B., Ferguson, M., Cherney, A., and Boreham, P. (June 2014). "Are Policy-Makers Interested in Social Research? Exploring the Sources and Uses of Valued Information among Public Servants in Australia." *Policy and Society, Contemporary Policy Work in Subnational States and NGOs,* 33(2), 89–101. doi:10.1016/j.polsoc.2014.04.004.

Hood, C. (1999). "The Garbage Can Model of Organization: Describing a Condition or Prescriptive Design Principle," in Egeberg, M. and Laegreid, P. (Eds.), *Organizing Political Institutions: Essays for Johan P. Olsen.* Oslo: Scandinavian University Press, pp. 59–78.

Hood, C. (2007). "What Happens When Transparency Meets Blame-Avoidance?" *Public Management Review*, 9(2), 191–210.

Howlett, M. (2007). "Analyzing Multi-Actor, Multi-Round Public Policy Decision-Making Processes in Government: Findings from Five Canadian Cases." *Canadian Journal of Political Science*, 40(3), 659–84.

Howlett, M. (2009). "Policy Analytical Capacity and Evidence-Based Policy-Making: Lessons from Canada." *Canadian Public Administration*, 52(2), 153–75.

Howlett, M. and Ramesh, M. (2003) *Studying Public Policy: Policy Cycles and Policy Subsystems*. Oxford: Oxford University Press.

Jacobs, A. S. (2008). "The Politics of When: Retribution, Investment and Policy Making for the Long Term." *British Journal of Political Science*, 38(2), 193–220.

John, P. (1998). *Analysing Public Policy*. London: Pinter.

Jones, B. D. (1994). *Re-Conceiving Decision-Making in Democratic Politics: Attention, Choice and Public Policy*. Chicago, IL: University of Chicago Press.

Kahler, M. (1989). "Organization and Cooperation: International Institutions and Policy Coordination." *Journal of Public Policy*, 8(3/4), 375–401.

Lester, J. P. and Stewart, J. (2000). *Public Policy: An Evolutionary Approach*. Belmont, CA: Wadsworth.

Lindblom, C. E. (1959). "The Science of Muddling Through." *Public Administration Review*, 19(2), 79–88.

Lindblom, C. E. (1977). *The Policy-Making Process*. New Haven, CT: Yale University Press.

MacRae Jr., D. and Wilde, J. A. (1985). *Policy Analysis for Public Decisions*. Lanham, MD: University Press of America.

MacRae, D. and Whittington, D. (1997). *Expert Advice for Policy Choice: Analysis and Discourse*. Washington DC: Georgetown University Press.

March, J. G. (1994). *A Primer on Decision-Making: How Decisions Happen*. New York: Free Press.

March, J. G., Olsen, J. P. and Weissinger-Baylon, R. (1986). "Garbage Can Models of Decision Making in Organizations," in March, J. G. and Weissinger-Baylon, Roger (Eds.), *Ambiguity and Command: Organizational Perspectives on Military Decision Making*. New York: Pitman Publishing, pp. 11–35.

Meyerson, M. and Banfield, E. C. (1955). *Politics, Planning, and the Public Interest: The Case of Public Housing in Chicago*. London: The Free Press of Glencoe.

Noveck, B. S. (2016). *Smart Citizens, Smarter State: The Technologies of Expertise and the Future of Governing*. Cambridge, MA: Harvard University Press.

Nutley, S. M., Walter, I., and Davies, H. T. O. (2007). *Using Evidence: How Research Can Inform Public Services*. Bristol, UK: Policy Press.

Parsons, W. (1995). *Public Policy: An Introduction to the Theory and Practice of Policy Analysis*. Cheltenham: Edward Elgar.

Patton, C. and Sawicki, D. (1993). *Basic Methods of Policy Analysis and Planning*. Upper Saddle River, NJ: Prentice Hall.

Pritchett, L. and Woolcock. M. (February 2004). "Solutions When the Solution Is the Problem: Arraying the Disarray in Development." *World Development, Part special issue: Island Studies*, 32(2), 191–212. doi:10.1016/j.worlddev. 2003.08.009.

Putt, A. and Springer, J. (1989). *Policy Research: Concepts, Methods, and Applications.* Upper Saddle River, NJ: Prentice Hall.

Quade, E.S. (1989). *Analysis for Public Decisions.* New York: Elsevier Science.

Quade, E.S. (1991). "Bounded Rationality and Organizational Learning." *Organization Science*, 2(1), 125–34.

Radin, B. A. and Boase, J. P. (2000). "Federalism, Political Structure, and Public Policy in the United States and Canada." *Journal of Comparative Policy Analysis*, 2(1), 65–90.

Richardson, H. S. (2002). *Democratic Autonomy: Public Reasoning About the Ends of Policy.* New York: Oxford University Press.

Sabatier, P. A. (Ed.). (1999). *Theories of the Policy Process.* Boulder, CT: Westview Press.

Scharpf, F. (1988). "The Joint Decision Trap: Lessons from German Federalism and European Integration." *Public Administration*, 66, 239–78.

Simon, H. A. (1957). *Administrative Behavior: A Study of Decision-Making Processes in Administrative Organization.* New York: Macmillan.

Simon, H. A. (1983). *Reason in Human Affairs.* Stanford, CA: Stanford University Press.

Steele, J. (October 2016). "Chilcot Report: Foreign Office." *The Political Quarterly*, 87(4), 484–5. doi:10.1111/1467–923X.12298.

Svara, J. H. (2006). "Complexity in Political-Administrative Relations and the Limits of the Dichotomy Concept." *Administrative Theory & Praxis*, 28(1), 121–39.

't Hart, P., Heyse, L., and Boin, A. (2001). "New Trends in Crisis Management Practice and Crisis Management Research: Setting the Agenda." *Journal of Contingencies and Crisis Management*, 9(4), 181–188. doi:10.1111/1468–5973.00168.

Teisman, G. R. (2000). "Models for Research into Decision-Making Processes: On Phases, Streams and Decision-Making Rounds." *Public Administration*, 78(4), 937–56.

Tummers, L. and Knies, E. (June 2016). "Measuring Public Leadership: Developing Scales for Four Key Public Leadership Roles." *Public Administration*, 94(2), 433–51. doi:10.1111/padm.12224.

Tversky, A. and Kahneman, D. (1986). "Rational Choice and the Framing of Decisions." *Journal of Business*, 59(4), Part 2: S251–S279.

Vining A. and Boardman, A. (2007). "The Choice of Formal Policy Methods in Canada," in Dobuzinskis, L., Howlett, M., and Laycock, D. (Eds.), *Policy Analysis in Canada.* Toronto: University of Toronto Press, pp. 48–85.

Walker, W. E., Vincent, A.W., Marchau, J., and Kwakkel, J. H. (2013). "Uncertainty in the Framework of Policy Analysis," in Thissen, W. A. H. and Walker, W. E. (Eds.), *Public Policy Analysis: New Developments.* New York: Springer, pp. 215–60.

Weimer, D. and Vining, A. (2011). *Policy Analysis: Concepts and Practice*. 5th edn. Upper Saddle River, NJ: Longman.

Weiss, C. H. (1980). "Knowledge Creep and Decision Accretion." *Knowledge: Creation, Diffusion, Utilization*, 1(3), 381–404.

Whiteman, D. (1985). "The Fate of Policy Analysis in Congressional Decision Making: Three Types of Use in Committees." *Western Political Quarterly*, 38(2), 294–311.

Zelditch, M., Harris, W., Thomas, G. M., and Walker, H. A. (1983). "Decisions, Nondecisions and Metadecisions." *Research in Social Movements, Conflict and Change*, 5, 1–32.

5 Policy implementation

Implementation occurs at a point in the policy process in which public policy decisions and plans that have heretofore existed largely as ideas are translated into actions. It has long been considered one of the most difficult, and critical, stages in the policy process for public managers. For it is the phase in which any deficiency in the ideas behind the design of the policy or any vulnerabilities with respect to the design itself and its impact upon the external environment, and vice versa, will become visible. Experienced public managers know that they will be ultimately judged on their ability to master the "art of getting things done," rather than by their good intentions.

This chapter offers an overview of the implementation challenges public managers face and how they can be overcome. It first explores the basics of policy implementation, including analytical approaches often used to manage its complexity. It then reviews typical implementation problems which managers face, before extracting lessons learned from the extensive literature on implementation for making implementation processes more adaptive and effective. In both diagnosing challenges and crafting strategies to overcome them, the chapter underlines two cross-cutting points. One is the need to build a concern for implementation into all phases of the policy process so as to avoid some of the most common negative pitfalls and consequences of policy fragmentation. The second is the importance of systematically considering the administrative and political contexts in which policy-making takes place in order to overcome many of the most common obstacles to effective implementation.

The basics of policy implementation

What is implementation? Why is it so complex?

Implementation is the activity in the policy process in which actors attempt to convert policy intentions and resources into actions resulting in specific policy outputs and ultimately in the achievement (or not) of intended policy outcomes. It can be seen as a form of network governance, since the defining characteristic of implementation is that it demands extensive coordination among a wide range of actors. This is particularly relevant where integration of multiple policy objectives is sought through a particular program.

Implementation is a high-stakes game. It exposes even well-formulated policies that have passed critical decision-making points to several acid tests—administrative feasibility and capacity, political and social acceptability, unforeseen consequences, a wide range of other contingencies—any of which can singly or in combination block policies from achieving their intended objectives. This makes it not only a difficult management challenge but also a potential source of blame and risk for both politicians and policymakers, both electorally and in terms of their career.

Each of the potential problems a policy may encounter has to be anticipated and carefully managed. But this is a difficult task. Failure to accurately anticipate implementation problems is the most common cause of policy failure. An "optimism bias," for example, often afflicts policymakers who assume that many problems will take care of themselves, or will never materialize at all, resulting occasionally in high-profile policy disasters and even more frequently in policies that perform far below expectation (Bovens and t'Hart 1996).

However, there are several reasons for the neglect of implementation issues, beyond unfounded optimism or hubris on the part of policy formulators and decision-makers. One key reason for the failure to incorporate implementation concerns into earlier phases of the policy process is the sheer complexity, both analytical and practical, that implementation poses. Policy implementation is a dynamic, not linear, process. Changing policy rarely involves a straightforward mobilization of the resources necessary to achieve well-defined policy aims that already have broad support. Instead, the implementation task can and often does involve elements of all the preceding "stages" of policy-making and all of the uncertainties and contingencies that these might entail.

Many questions arise primarily in other parts of the policy process, such as:

- Where did the impetus for the policy come from?
- Who decided on it, how and why?
- What is the nature of the policy benefits, and to whom do they accrue?
- What is the nature of the costs of the policy reform, and who bears them?
- How complex are the changes being put into practice?

These all affect the way in which implementation plays out in practice. In addition, the implementation stage may influence other "stages" of the process, as when it involves interpretation and negotiation of policy aims (as in the policy formulation stage), or when implementers make decisions among significantly different administrative and program design alternatives that may affect the type of policy outcomes actually produced and their reception among key players in the policy community.

This latter concern is another key factor in implementation success and failure: the sheer number of actors involved the process of delivering services to citizens, in areas such as pensions or health care, or in regulating activities such as crime or substance abuse. Implementation affects, and is affected by, a multitude of actors who continue to (re-)define problems and solutions in a given policy domain; and these may include actors who were only marginal players in previous policy formulation and decision-making activities but who later come to the fore as the policy is put into motion (May 2003). Relatively minor administrative issues, such as the failure to prevent some minor abuses of food stamp programs, may be used as reasons to re-litigate earlier policy work and attack the goals and objectives behind the program as a whole.

Despite this plethora of players, however, the bureaucracy is always a significant actor in, and decisive factor underpinning, policy implementation, whether it plays the role of overseeing other actors or itself delivers services. The usual form of government agency involved in implementation is the *ministry* or *department* at the central level, and different agencies at lower levels of government (state, provincial, or local) each bring their own interests, ambitions, and traditions. But other organizational forms such as *tribunals* or *commissions*, which can in a number of jurisdictions and circumstances perform quasi-judicial functions (including appeals concerning licensing, certification of personnel or programs, and issue of permits), can also be key implementers. They may hold administrative or public hearings to aid them in their activities and interact frequently with the public and interest groups in the design and redesign of programs and practices.

On the other side of this relationship are these affected publics and groups that are the *target groups* of policies—that is, groups whose behavior is intended or expected to be altered by government action. They play a major direct and indirect role in the implementation process as well. One way they do so is relatively passive—the way in which they accept or reject and resist against a given policy or program. But they may also play a more active and direct role in service delivery through, for example, various kinds of co-production arrangements of the type discussed in Chapter 3. The political and economic resources of these target groups, and how they can be mobilized to support or block agency action, have major effects on the implementation of policies. It is therefore quite common for regulators to strike compromises with these groups, or attempt to use the groups' own resources in some cases, to make the task of implementation simpler or less expensive than continually having to go to the courts to settle administrative and other issues.

A third reason for the neglect of implementation issues lies in its political sensitivity. The implementation process itself not only creates winners and losers, it is also the stage in the policy process where the stakes of winning or losing begin to manifest themselves very clearly to many participants whose interests and desires may have been left out of earlier stages of the process (see Box 5.1). Agencies, and even divisions within agencies, may continue to compete for resources and control over implementation activities; and tensions may arise between the public, private, and non-profit organizations as they vie for influence and funds to implement government programs.

Box 5.1: Implementation as politics by other means

What happens to major public interest-oriented legislation, typically enacted with great acclaim and controversy, *after* they are enacted? This is the question asked of US reforms over the last thirty years by Eric Patashnik in his book *Reforms at Risk*. Patashnik reveals multiple, reinforcing threats to reform sustainability in this implementation phase, arising from the political dynamics. Narrow interests that have lost out in a general-interest reform process reassert themselves when public attention shifts away from the legislation. Reform success then depends on whether the power basis of narrowly configured interest groups can be disabled, and new social actors—the beneficiaries of reforms—can be better organized to safeguard reform success. A tall order.

The implementation of the Tax Reform Act (TRA) of 1986 is a case in point. TRA aimed to rationalize the tax code, reducing special interest tax loopholes and shutting down tax havens that only benefited the rich and large corporate interests. A special set of circumstances, including skillful political entrepreneurship among proponents, led to passage of a surprisingly strong act; but within a few years many of its gains had been eroded by the creation of new tax breaks and the emergence of new forms of tax shelters. The basic explanation Patashnik gives is that the reforms failed to change the influence of lobbyists or make a significant dent in the political incentives associated with the granting of tax favors. The game that spawned the problem continued to be played in much the same way after the temporary and passing influence of the Act.

A more successful example of reform sustainability involves the implementation success of Indonesia's governmental anti-corruption commission, the KPK, since its launch in 2002. Established in the aftermath of the fall of authoritarian President Suharto, the commission has successfully investigated and prosecuted hundreds of senior bureaucrats and parliamentarians from all political parties; for this reason, many analysts consider it the most successful anti-corruption commission in a developing country setting. In the process, the KPK earned powerful enemies, such that it faced repeated efforts to defang its broad powers, variously through the appointment of weak commissioners, defunding of its budget, or removal of particular investigative powers. The KPK has generally been able to protect itself from such rearguard actions through proactive public support (it has the highest public approval rating of any government ministry in Indonesia), galvanized by social media and by a newly revitalized civil society sector with dozens of anti-corruption watchdog NGOs. Though political battles over the KPK continue, it represents a case in which the reconfiguration of political and social forces has helped sustain high-performance implementation over more than a decade.

In policy formulation and even decision-making, critical differences between stakeholders may be papered over by using vague language or even postponing outright decisions on mission-critical but politically or bureaucratically "sensitive" aspects of policies. This has the advantage of keeping a policy process moving forward and "buying time" for more supportive coalitions to be built. But the consequences of such avoidance become unavoidable during the implementation stage, in which public managers will struggle to generate, allocate and control resources, and interpret policy intentions. The intended outputs and results of a policy will fail to materialize, while negative side-effects of policies will become more evident.

While implementation sometimes finds the high-publicity politics of policy adoption coming back with a vengeance, many policies witness a decline in public attention after a policy decision has been made. This has the effect of giving greater opportunity to administrators and/or well-organized special interests to vary the original intent of a decision should they so desire.

"Top-down" and "bottom-up" approaches to understanding implementation

The set of tasks practically associated with implementation is best understood as a "continuum of strategic and operational task functions" (Brinkerhoff and Crosby 2002: 25). Tasks related to implementation must be integrated throughout the policy process, from high-level strategic design considerations (such as constituency building) to concurrent operational-level design and capacity-building tasks (such as project management). Failing this integration, large gaps are likely to loom between policy intentions and actual execution.

Two of the academic founders of the study of implementation, Jeffrey Pressman and Aaron Wildavsky, captured the mood of early implementation research in the subtitle to their classic text *Implementation* (Pressman and Wildavsky 1973): "How great expectations in Washington are dashed in Oakland; Or, Why it's amazing that federal programs work at all." While we wish to avoid giving the impression that effective implementation is impossible, it is undoubtedly important to squarely face its difficulties.

There are two basic vantage points from which to view the gap between policy intentions and implementation practices and outcomes. The first perspective sees implementation from the viewpoint of high-level policymakers attempting to control outcomes at the grassroots. This so-called "top-down" view can be described as a "correspondence" theory of implementation in that it assumes a clear articulation of the intended policy and that the main conceptual and practical difficulty lies in how to transmit this intention faithfully down the line of bureaucratic command. Deviations at the field level from the intentions of policymakers count as an implementation "gap" or "deficit" which can be corrected or controlled but only through various mechanisms—such as audits and inspections—designed to allow "principles" to control "agents" in the field. Theorists adopting this perspective look for deficiencies in the way policies are communicated, and at standards and practices of implementation enforcement, from policymakers to field-level implementers (Ellig et al. 1995).

"Bottom-up" analysts, in contrast, begin with the assumption that "street-level" bureaucrats often face an impossible task in attempting to faithfully reproduce superior's aims into changes on the ground and instead "make do" as best they can, altering components of policies "on the fly" in order to achieve some goals and objectives while others may be ignored or set aside (Lipsky 1980). Policy ambiguity, limited resources, and time pressures may make it impossible to implement policies as intended. To the extent that outcomes are deemed less than satisfactory from a policymaker's point of view, this perspective looks for the reasons in resource gaps, in the incentives embedded in the institutional environment faced by street-level bureaucrats, and in the understanding of their work and roles that develop in response to often untenable implementation requirements.

Figure 5.1 presents a model of implementation drawing on both bottom-up and top-down perspectives—one that may help policy actors think through the variables that can affect implementation. It outlines five categories of variables linking policy formation on the left side to implementation outputs and outcomes on the right. It places heavy emphasis on the "disposition of implementers," i.e. the cognitive maps, incentives, and resources available to those ultimately responsible for implementing the most important provisions of the policy. Each of the following categories can be expressed as a set of questions that policy actors can use to help identify implementation problems.

1. *Policy design.* Within the policy design category, we can distinguish between policy content and resources available for implementation. Are clear, consistent statements of objectives and criteria for successful implementation provided in the legal framework underpinning the policy? And are resources sufficient for successful implementation made available, or a plan for resource mobilization in place?

2. *Inter-organizational communication and enforcement activities.* This category asks how the policy is communicated to lower levels, and within what framework of accountability? What levels of communication and enforcement effort is present?

3. *Characteristics of the implementing agencies/disposition of implementers.* The institutional characteristics of implementing agencies have a profound effect on how lower levels perceive and act on upper-level directives. The disposition of individual implementers is closely linked to the characteristics of agencies in which they are embedded. It is also affected by the possibility that the implementors may face conflicts between their official duties and their personal interests. For instance, they may have opportunities to moonlight (to earn non-official income) while on the job—think of a rural health clinic doctor who has a private practice on the side, using the same facilities—or work within environments plagued by outright corruption. This category thus delineates key aspects of agency culture and accountability relationships.

4. *Implementation outputs and outcomes/impacts.* The three categories above jointly determine implementation outputs, which are linked to impacts on the defined problem via their "policy logic." In other words, are there logically substantiated links between policy outputs— assuming perfect implementation—and the problems the policy is meant to address?

5. *Policy learning.* In reading Figure 5.1, the feedback loops on the borders are important, as they make the model dynamic. The lower feedback loop concerns *policy learning.* The assumption is that programs may be re-designed both at key intervals in a formal process (the loop leading to policy redesign) and in a more informal, iterative process as local implementers adjust their expectations and behavior to the actual implementation situation they face (the arrow leading to implementer disposition).

6. *Action environment.* The upper feedback loop is via the *action environment* to all three of the determinants of implementation noted above. The action environment is here broken into components such as the

public sector institutional environment, political support, and social and economic factors. (All of these must be defined within the parameters of the policy at hand.) The influence of this environment lies in two areas. It structures or influences the formation of the policy in the first place. But there is a more dynamic sense as well. As policies work themselves out in a given environment, they may affect the environment in ways that change—for the better or worse, depending on the perspective taken, and in intended or unintended ways—those action environment influences on implementation. For example, a program may over time empower a previously marginalized group to have a greater stake in a particular policy, changing the stakeholder alignment in ways that create new support or opposition to a policy.

The conceptual framework presented here is a way of structuring inquiry into observed implementation patterns of a particular policy. It incorporates some elements of both classically "top-down" and "bottom-up" approaches. The framework can be used to identify specific implementation constraints (as the top-down model stresses), but focuses much attention onto the institutional environment at the local level and the dynamic impacts (often unpredicted) of implementation.

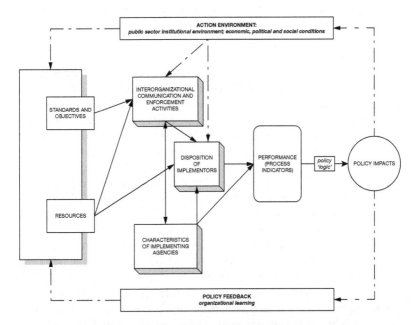

Figure 5.1 Integrating top-down and bottom-up perspectives in implementation

Sources: Van Meter and Van Horn, 1975; Hill and Hupe, 2002:186; Fritzen, 2000:1

The importance of understanding context

How these top-down and bottom-up practices play out in a specific case depends very much on the issue involved and the institutional context in which implementation takes place (Hjern 1982). Long-term factors such as administrative traditions and styles of decision-making as well as the nature of administrative recruitment and merit systems play a heavy role in conditioning the environment in which both top-down and bottom-up activity occurs (Knill 1999). It is very important for policy managers and implementers, and others, to be aware of these structures and practices when assessing these potential obstacles to effective implementation, and when drawing appropriate implications for action (Howlett 2003).

While a plethora of contextual factors may be important to a given case, four warrant special attention. The first is the *degree of political and policy stability* present in the policy system. The environment for policy implementation may be considered "enabling" if there is relatively strong political support for the program outputs that are to be produced, and if bureaucratic capacity for analytical and implementation tasks is relatively strong (Matland 1995).

A second is the *degree of environmental turbulence*, or the extent to which the external political and economic environment in which policymakers are working is changing slowly or more rapidly. When an environment is "turbulent" it may be appropriate to alter bureaucratic routines and program parameters much more quickly than in more stable environments (Hill and Hupe 2002). In relatively stable circumstances, coordinators of policy implementation may have more opportunities to build network capacities that will facilitate more integrated implementation especially if they are able to identify and build strong coalitions supporting integrated policy-making in a given thematic area. Where change is fast, their approach will of necessity need to be nimble, even "entrepreneurial," looking for entry points that can serve to focus political attention onto areas for rapid action. Where the political and policy environment is more stable, building bridges to a wide variety of potential partners and focusing on overall network capacity may be the most suitable implementation strategy (the "partnering" approach).

How these first two factors—a facilitative general policy environment and the pace of change—intersect offer clues for implementation prospects, which Figure 5.2 summarizes. Where the environment is not particularly facilitative, and where change (economic, social, or political) is rapid and unfavorable, public managers are likely to be restricted to "damage control" —keeping open the possibility of a more integrated and effective approach to implementation when the environment for it becomes more tenable. With greater stability in the environment, public managers may be relegated to "coping" or, at best, "scheming"; that is, identifying interventions to target

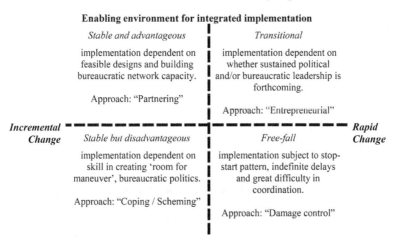

Enabling environment for integrated implementation

Stable and advantageous	*Transitional*
implementation dependent on feasible designs and building bureaucratic network capacity. Approach: "Partnering"	implementation dependent on whether sustained political and/or bureaucratic leadership is forthcoming. Approach: "Entrepreneurial"

Incremental Change ━━━━━━━━━━━━━━━━━━━━━━━━━━━ *Rapid Change*

Stable but disadvantageous	*Free-fall*
implementation dependent on skill in creating 'room for maneuver', bureaucratic politics. Approach: "Coping / Scheming"	implementation subject to stop-start pattern, indefinite delays and great difficulty in coordination. Approach: "Damage control"

Disabling environment for integrated implementation

Figure 5.2 A typology of institutional change environments as they may affect implementation

Source: Fritzen, 2007

for implementation that can serve as stepping stones of a longer-term, more ambitious approach should circumstances change. Where political currents are unsupportive of policy change initiatives even after official adoption, implementation may have to "fly under the radar," keeping the initial content as low key and technical (non-overtly political) as possible, as they look for allies and wait for conditions to change. Where to look for such opportunities—how ambitious one can be during adverse times and in adverse environments—is a difficult question to answer in the abstract; but careful delineation of different stakeholders and their interests, as suggested below, may offer useful cues.

A third contextual factor concerns the openness of the policy process— the degree to which the process is being influenced by a range of actors rather than having a narrow decision-making base. For instance, in a highly pluralistic country with a strong nongovernmental sector and a free press, policy-making will inevitably be shaped by a broader range of actors than a country in which policy-making is restricted to a small elite. This distinction has important practical implications for implementation. In more democratic, open polities, conflicts at the stage of agenda-setting, policy formulation, and decision-making are likely to be relatively more transparent and regularized. This may imply that proponents and opponents of policies will be better identified—and may have reached more sustainable compromises built into the policy itself—by the implementation stage. In countries in which political decision-making is less formally contested, the politics of implementation may instead become "hotter," as actors who were excluded from decision-making strive to deflect policies with which they do not agree, or to steer them in a more acceptable direction, diverting them from their original objectives.

Finally, the degree of public sector decentralization is another contextual element that will almost always be relevant to consider in policy implementation. Decentralization is one of the catch-words of the development debates of recent decades, with most countries implementing, or at least endorsing, the idea of passing enhanced resources and authorities down to lower levels of governments (territorial decentralization) or to nontraditional, reconstituted authorities (functional decentralization). The extent to which such trends are present will affect the way decisions regarding policy adoption are reached, resources mobilized, and administrative and non-bureaucratic actors coordinated for implementation (see Table 5.1).

Regardless of the extent of decentralization in a country, however, central-level actors—in many settings the most likely coordinators—will need to fulfill highly important functions: steering decision-making, monitoring

Table 5.1 Center-local relations as they impact on implementation

Nature of decentralization	*Basis for decentralization, and Implications for policy implementation*	
	Territorial	*Functional*
Within formal political structures	Devolution (political decentralization, local government, democratic decentralization); *need to work with local governments in agenda-setting/decision-making, and to strengthen capacity/ political accountability*	Interest group representation; *potential to incorporate variety of interest groups into decision-making forums for intersectoral development*
Within public administrative or parastatal structures	Deconcentration (administrative decentralization, field administration); *raises coordination requirements and potential for conflicts across sectors and between levels of government*	Establishment of parastatals and quangos; *Potential to establish separate administrative authorities with integrated policy-making or execution responsibilities in a particular policy domain*

Source: Adapted from Turner and Hulme, 1997

implementation, setting and enforcing minimum standards, and providing technical assistance and capacity-building where local capacities vary significantly (as they usually do). However, particularly in newly decentralizing systems, central actors are not always well primed or incentivized to play these essential roles. Box 5.2 provides one example of this challenge.

Box 5.2: Implementation and institutional change

Implementation is often affected by broader institutional changes affecting a country or sector. For example, health ministry authorities across developing countries have struggled to cope with decentralization trends affecting the implementation of social service provision. This is particularly true in countries experiencing a transition from centrally planned to market economies.

Consider successive generations of health sector reforms in Vietnam. Before it began its transition to a predominantly market-oriented economy in the mid-1980s, the grassroots level of the health sector included some 10,000 primary health care clinics dispersed across local governments throughout the country. They were staffed by paraprofessionals— so-called "barefoot doctors" (often nurses)—paid for by each commune collective, the backbone of Vietnam's economy. The collapse of the collectives and the introduction of market-oriented reforms brought organizational and fiscal disarray to this grassroots health network.

In a first phase of reform, lasting roughly to the mid-1990s, clinics responded to the disarray by trying to raise operating funds through a combination of initially unregulated user fees, and highly uneven local government support. Gradually, as the economy took off through the 1990s, the central government brought the funding of basic salaries under its budget, invested heavily in specific health programs (anti-tuberculosis, control of diarrheal diseases etc.) and secured donor funding to rebuild the crumbling infrastructure at the grassroots. Central authorities also tried to curb the use of rampant user fees and bribes in medical facilities. Despite some success, inequalities in access to care widened over the decade, and a new round of reforms aimed at the expansion of health insurance and the better training and supervision of local health personnel.

Through all of these changes, both clinics and central authorities faced difficulties in adapting to their new roles in an increasingly complex health care system.

Challenges in policy implementation

"Perfect implementation" and the anatomy of failure

One way of looking at implementation challenges is to assess what it would take to achieve so-called "perfect" implementation and then determine how these can be overcome. According to an influential exposition, Hogwood and Gunn (1993) identified ten "preconditions for implementation success":

- circumstances external to the implementing agency do not impose crippling constraints;
- adequate time and sufficient resources are made available to the program;
- the required combination of resources is available;
- the policy to be implemented is based on a valid theory of cause and effect;
- the relationship between cause and effect is direct and that; there are few, if any intervening links;
- the dependency relationships are minimal;
- there is agreement of, and understanding on, objectives;
- the tasks are fully specified in correct sequence;
- there is perfect communication and coordination;
- those in authority can demand and obtain perfect compliance.

Examining these preconditions for success can help us categorize some of the main conditions that may typically *obstruct* an implementation process. Table 5.2 uses the same three broad categories of analysis and action emphasized in other chapters of this book—the need to develop a coherent set of objectives for integrated policy-making, strong support, and authorization for their implementation, and sufficient operational capacity to get the job done—to examine typical implementation constraints.

The first broad category of conditions obstructing implementation is *mission-related*. The poor design of interventions implies that policies may fail even if implemented as intended. Or goals adopted in a multisectoral process may be too vague to meaningfully translate into operational programs and interventions.

A second category of difficulties involves the lack of adequate bureaucratic and political *support* for implementation. Support for policies can often stop at the rhetorical level, or at the agencies or levels of government that initiated them. Lower levels of government, and grassroots actors on whom actual implementation success hinges, may discover that they have little

Table 5.2 Typical implementation barriers

Problem	Description
Political (support and authorization) barriers	
Slow authorization	Plans and resource mobilization proceed very slowly due to the existence of multiple-veto points among stakeholders in a network, making forward progress difficult.
Weak political support	Plans may proceed and even attain moderate levels of success in the pilot project stage while flying under the "radar" of key politicians with opposing interests, until program begins to "scale up."
Bureaucratic opposition	Key players in the interagency network tasked with implementing policy slow or sabotage implementation due to low priority of project, lacking incentives, and/or competing interests.
Poor implementer incentives	Local implementers (local government coordinating executives or front-line staff of agencies), who were not consulted during the decision-making stage, have inadequate "buy-in" or incentives to comply with directives from below.
Analytical competence barriers	
Vague or multiple missions	Intersectoral nature of plans and implementation leads to papering over conflicting goals or not clearly specifying trade-offs in operational terms.
Changing priorities	Trade-offs made in policy decision-making, e.g. between environmental and economic dimensions of a policy problem, may need to be reconsidered in light of changing economic and political conditions.
Poor design	Social or environmental programs that are unlikely to work as intended given multiple constraints left unaddressed by program design; failure is "overdetermined"—i.e. will occur if any of the constraints are left unaddressed.
Uneven feasibility	Different components of the integrated plans may be operationally linked—one can only advance if all are jointly present—subjecting operations to the "weakest link."
Operational capacity barriers	
Fund limitations	Funds necessary to implement approved plans slow to materialize, blocking progress, while in the meantime key elements of situation change "facts on the ground" and/or initial supporters of the effort lose heart and abandon effort.

continued

Table 5.2 continued

Problem	Description
Weak management structure or network coordination capacity	Poor precedents for coordination between major agencies—exacerbated in case of intersectoral partnerships—makes routine decisions slow and implementation dysfunctional.
Lack of clarity in operational plans	Approved and funded plans are mismanaged due to poor specification of roles, responsibilities, and accountability. Often made worse by poor oversight and information systems with which to hold implementers accountable and make course corrections.

understanding of, or stake in, the policies they are asked to execute. Initial implementation may also trigger resistance to an integrated plan that might not have been predicted at the beginning of the process, particularly if not all relevant stakeholders had been consulted. "Political will" may begin to evaporate when difficult trade-offs need to be made in practice, not just on paper, and as constituencies negatively affected by policy trade-offs raise their voices (or even flex their muscles).

Finally, a range of *capacity*-related difficulties may have negative repercussions on implementation. Operational capacity is the bedrock of implementation. Many—perhaps most—ambitious attempts at integrated planning stop at the level of paper plans. The multiple types of capacity necessary to implement these plans often go ignored, or are optimistically subsumed under the heading of "capacity-building requirements." Capacity includes human and financial resources, the institutional arrangements and procedures that underpin policies and ensure consistent delivery, and even the social capacities that help determine how social groupings will respond to implementation initiatives.

While all of these capacity requirements may be underestimated by public managers initially, implementation is particularly vulnerable to deficiencies in *network coordination capacity*—the ability of organizations to work together to achieve a common outcome. Coordination across agencies and—an even greater challenge—across sectors for implementation may be required in several different forms, such as sharing information, pooling resources, and (where activities fall outside the traditional gambit of any one organization) jointly implementing assigned tasks. Yet, coordination must overcome several common obstacles, well established in the literature, including the perceived threat agencies may feel to their autonomy from working together and the confusion or conflict over the nature of the task that stems from the inherently complicated, multisectoral nature of goal-setting (Agranoff and McGuire 1999).

Strategies for public managers in policy implementation

We now turn to specific strategies that can help policy actors to manage these challenges.

Design policies with implementation in mind

The first recommendation looks back to issues first raised in Chapter 3. Implementation considerations should be incorporated directly into the formulation stage of any policy (Lindquist 2006). This is particularly important where policies are long term in their approach.

There are several ways to do this. One is by starting relatively small while building support for more integrated policies. This will be warranted when the key issues are contested or beset by grave uncertainties. There is a range of unknowns at the outset of any complex initiative for policy change, not least regarding the incentives faced by, and inclinations of, the different actors who must work together. Thus, conceiving smaller-scale initiatives as "policy experiments" can help facilitate adaptive implementation—the ability to learn what works, and how to fix what isn't working, in the process of implementation itself. The design of projects as adaptive policy experiments implies the existence of strong information systems, a point reinforced throughout this book (Stoker and John 2009; Vreugdenhil 2012).

Another key to the proper design of policies from an implementation perspective is to systematically review their logical construction *prior* to the implementation stage itself. The basic intention is to test the degree to which policies are logically constructed so that invested inputs stand a realistic chance of being processed into project outputs, which themselves contribute reliably to the required outcomes. "Forward mapping" and "backward mapping" are two related tools that may assist in the attempt to ensure policies are logically and soundly designed to achieve their stated aims, and that all the elements required for implementation are "assembled" and in place (see Box 5.3).

Get operational fast while mobilizing resources creatively

The implementation tasks facing leaders and managers involve:

- *identifying* individuals and units within organizations that will carry forward specific plans and collaborations;

Box 5.3: Forward and backward mapping in implementation design

In forward mapping, otherwise known as scenario analysis, the analyst writes out for him or herself how implementation is implicitly *supposed* to take place (if it is to be successful), including all the relevant actors, their roles, and the sequence and orchestration of their actions. The analyst then uses this narrative as the basis for two fundamental critiques:

- Critique 1: Is each of the actors actually likely to be sufficiently incentivized and capable of acting in the manner prescribed?

- Critique 2: Might any *other* actor affected by the policy get involved and potentially interfere with or deflect policy intentions during implementation, and if so, can they actually be stopped from doing so?

Based on the answers to these questions, the analyst then rewrites the scenario to make it more realistic, including preventive and other measures to enhance the likelihood of success.

Backward mapping—sometimes labeled "bottom-up policy design"— involves first specifying the actual behaviors that need to take place in order that policy outcomes will be achieved. For instance, in order to achieve the policy goal of cleaning up city canals, one might specify the behavioral change that "city inhabitants no longer throw their garbage into the canal." Having identified the specific behaviors to be changed, the analyst *then* designs policies from different logical options that can help achieve this objective, paying special attention to how the intervention can practically motivate the required changes in behavior.

These analytical tools are in some ways quite commonsensical and straightforward. But they may prove surprisingly useful in anticipating policy implementation problems, and in brainstorming alternative policy options to increase the likelihood of success in implementation.

Source: D. Weimer and A. Vining (1992) *Policy Analysis: Concepts and Practice*, Englewood Cliffs, NJ: Prentice Hall, pp. 402–6

- *operationalizing* broad policy objectives into specific, measurable targets that, in turn, are broken down into supporting tasks implemented by identifiable groups of people on a schedule;
- *ensuring necessary operational capacity*, including attention not just to equipment and human resources but also to the incentives for grass-roots

implementers to act as required for successful execution of the policy intention (Agranoff 2008).

To make the leap from developing a coherent policy design to implementation demands *operational planning*. Operational planning is the process of developing initial and intermediate objectives and implementation targets for the interrelated interventions that make up complex policy change initiatives. Tasks need to be linked with specific agencies, and if possible individuals, as well as financial resources; implementation guidelines necessary for the effective interpretation of policies are also typically required.

Ultimately, policies and programs supporting an implementation plan must be integrated into normal budget cycles and operations. Before this can happen, coordinators of such efforts will have to be creative and entrepreneurial in identifying a range of sources of the resources necessary to get initial efforts off the ground. Resources necessary and sufficient for effective implementation rarely "report for duty" simply because agreement has been reached on some policy objectives. More often, they must be mobilized from a variety of sources, in a process that can determine to large extent how effective and timely implementation proceeds. A recommended approach is to view resource mobilization as a constant and continuing implementation challenge rather than a one-off task (Brinkerhoff and Crosby 2002).

An initial challenge in this context is the identification of "seed" or "bridge" financing and allocations of personnel that can enable integrated policy-making and implementation to get off the ground and initial activities to begin. To secure such initial financing often requires negotiations with a range of actors, including government budget authorities and potential external partners. In the longer term, securing more stable sources of fiscal and other necessary resources often comes from initial demonstrations of success (enhancing the ease and attractiveness of such efforts to key stakeholders) coupled with a more official, legally grounded framework for the initiative and its continued implementation.

Invest early and heavily in building capacity within implementation networks

The defining characteristic of contemporary policy implementation is that it demands extensive coordination among an unusually wide range of actors. No single agency can be responsible for most implementation activities, and that the coordinators of implementation should be prepared to grapple with a serious degree of *confusion* (because of the large number of stakeholders) and *conflict* (among stakeholders who share some interests and compete in others) during the implementation process (Goldsmith and Eggers 2004).

There are several dimensions to the capacity-building challenge for network implementation. One is to decide on the appropriate structure to underpin implementation. Key options mirror those for the decision-making forums noted earlier, including allocating integrated implementation tasks to an ad hoc task force, an existing agency that takes on a slightly different set of tasks, or to a nongovernmental or private market unit via delegation or contracting.

Another network capacity-building challenge is to develop—and use—effective accountability and management systems within the network. Accountability needs to be underpinned by an agreement on performance indicators as well as effective information systems that reliably update stakeholders and managers on the state of targeted outputs. Effective accountability must be linked to the mobilization of incentives and disincentives sufficient to motivate an acceptably high level of implementation effort. These are the classic instruments of hierarchical management, but remain equally relevant in an age of network management.

Yet accountability can only partly rely on such formal measures. The capacity of networks to implement policy-making in an integrated fashion will also rely on the density of relationships—the "social capital"—among local actors (such as NGOs, communities, local government coordinators, and line agencies).

Manage the dynamic process of change

Perhaps the most fundamental advice that can be offered to public managers regarding implementation can be summed up as follows: be aware of, and prepared for, the complex stakeholder dynamics you will face. Implementation of complex policy initiatives is *fundamentally* a challenge of coordination. While coordination has a number of requirements, the prerequisite for dealing effectively with any of them is a thorough understanding of stakeholder interests, resources, and perceptions (Fenwick and McMillan 2010).

Stakeholder analysis can serve as a basic analytical aid in this context. There are a wide variety of formats and variations on stakeholder analysis, but they share some common features: the delineation of all actors potentially concerned by, interested in, important to, or having any power over the projects being initiated. Such analyses also involve consideration of these actors' interests, level of organization, resources and capacities, and options for action (Glicken 2000).

To keep stakeholder dynamics on track during implementation is fundamentally part of a "change management" strategy. The challenge of avoiding the change management mistakes shown in Box 5.4, which was based on

---

Box 5.4: Eight change management mistakes to avoid

In "Why Transformation Efforts Fail," John Kotter laid out eight "errors" that are admirably self-explanatory. They were:

Not establishing a great enough sense of urgency (Kotter argues most non-incremental change only takes place when the need for it is acutely felt);

Not creating a powerful enough guiding coalition (involving all the senior leadership of an organization, who lay their personal reputations on the line in pursuing change);

Lacking a vision (particularly one that is "relatively easy to communicate and appeals to customers, stockholders and employees");

Undercommunicating the vision by a factor of ten (by which he means to emphasize that gaining "understanding and support" among thousands of potential individuals for the change effort to succeed can only be done with a huge effort to communicate effectively);

Not removing obstacles to the new vision (such as inappropriate organizational structure or key personnel who are opposed);

Not systematically planning for and creating short-term wins (much needed, he argues, to gain momentum for deeper reforms that often have high up-front costs);

Declaring victory too soon (often after only months or a few years, when in fact change efforts often need to last "five to ten years" before they "sink deeply into a company's culture"); and

Not anchoring changes in the corporation's culture (making the change vulnerable to reversal when the initial conditions and pressures subside).

Source: Kotter, 2007

---

work with private sector corporations, is great; but that in the public sector is even greater. In the public sector, the leadership that would be able to articulate such a "coherent vision" and "sense of urgency" underscoring implementation efforts, and the implementation setting itself, are both likely to be more fragmented and contested.

Conclusion: policy implementation as successful network management

There is never likely to be a "single best practice" associated with the implementation of complex policy initiatives, given the great diversity of country contexts, sectors, and problems involved. But this chapter has underlined some of the ways in which coordinators of such reforms can improve their chances of implementation success. Policy managers need to:

• be prepared for the implementation challenge by using several analytical tools, such as stakeholder analysis and the consideration of the balance of center and local roles in implementation
• have a strategic roadmap for iteratively generating increased support and resources in the implementation process itself
• develop effective managerial and accountability systems that are facilitative of "network capacity," which is likely to be the critical capacity necessary in multi-stakeholder implementation challenges.

For policy managers to play these roles, they will have to continuously develop their skills along a number of dimensions. These far exceed the technical. As an experienced practitioner recently remarked:

> Anyone attempting to exercise leadership in important policy matters . . . . must develop certain competencies that include a plan that calls for attending to conceiving and articulating a vision and a philosophy that support a comprehensive change process, assembling and motivating reliable partners as stakeholders in the process, understanding the cultural and communication skills necessary for the completion of the tasks involved, securing the political support by stakeholders through public engagement using publicity for the process and the outcomes, and finally insuring continuity by promoting mentoring of new leaders for the next phase of development.
>
> (Southard, 2016: 5)

What is striking about Southard's view of competencies is the way in which implementation concerns stretch well beyond a particular "phase" of the policy process. Policy managers should not take a narrow view of implementation as a technical control. Rather, they should be primed to identify and cope with the multiple ways in which ongoing political tensions, goal ambiguities, and the stakeholder all shape adaptive implementation efforts.

Once a policy or program has been put into place, of course, conditions and personnel change and with them the nature of the outputs and outcomes the program or policy can deliver. Public managers must be involved in the continual monitoring and evaluation, if learning is to be effective and policies are to be adapted to move towards policy success. These subjects are addressed in Chapter 6.

References

Bardach, E. (1977). *The Implementation Game: What Happens After a Bill Becomes a Law*. Cambridge, MA: MIT Press.

Agranoff, R. and McGuire, M. (1999). "Managing in Network Settings." *Policy Studies Review*, 16(1), 18–41.

Agranoff, Robert (March 2008). "Enhancing Performance Through Public Sector Networks: Mobilizing Human Capital in Communities of Practice." *Public Performance & Management Review*, 31(3), 320–47. doi:10.2753/PMR1530-9576310301.

Barrett, S. M. (2004). "Implementation Studies: Time for a Revival? Personal Reflections on 20 Years of Implementation Studies." *Public Administration*, 82(2), 249–62.

Bovens, M. and t'Hart, P. (1996). *Understanding Policy Fiascoes*. New Brunswick, NJ: Transaction Press.

Brinkerhoff, D. W. and Crosby, B. L. (2002). *Managing Policy Reform: Concepts and Tools for Decision-Makers in Developing and Transitional Countries*. Bloomfield, PA: Kumarian Press.

Brusca, I. and Montesinos, V. (2016). "Implementing Performance Reporting in Local Government: A Cross-Countries Comparison." *Public Performance & Management Review*, 39(3), 506–34.

Cashore, B. and Howlett, M. (2006). "Behavioural Thresholds and Institutional Rigidities as Explanations of Punctuated Equilibrium Processes in Pacific Northwest Forest Policy Dynamics," in Repute, R. (Ed.), *Punctuated Equilibrium and the Dynamics of U.S. Environmental Policy*, Yale, CT: Yale University Press, pp. 137–61.

Department of the Prime Minister and Cabinet, Australian Government (2014) Successful Implementation of Policy Initiatives. Commonwealth of Australia. Available online at www.anao.gov.au/work/better-practice-guide/successful-implementation-policy-initiatives, accessed March 24, 2016.

Ellig, J., Lavoie, D., and Foss, P. (1995). "The Principle-Agent Relationship in Organizations," in Foss, P. (Ed.), *Economic Approaches to Organizations and Institutions: An Introduction*. Aldershot, UK: Dartmouth.

Fenwick, J. and McMillan, J. (2010). *Public Management in the Postmodern Era: Challenges and Prospects*. Cheltenham, UK: Edward Elgar Publishing, 2010.

Fritzen, S. (2000). Decentralization and local government performance: A comparative framework with application to social policy reform in Vietnam. Ph.D. Dissertation. Princeton University, Princeton.

Fritzen, S. (2007). "Linking Context and Strategy in Donor Support for Decentralisation: A Diagnostic Framework." *Public Administration and Development*, 27.1, 13–25.

Glicken, J. (2000). "Getting Stakeholder Participation 'Right': A Discussion of Participatory Processes and Possible Pitfalls." *Environmental Science and Policy*, 3, 305–10.

Goldsmith, S. and Eggers, W. D. (2004). *Governing by Network: The New Shape of the Public Sector*. Washington DC: Brookings Institution Press.

Griddle, M. S. and Thomas, J. W. (1991). *Public Choices and Policy Change: The Political Economy of Reform in Developing Countries.* Baltimore, MD: John Hopkins University Press.

Hall, P. (1993). "Policy Paradigms, Social Learning, and the State: The Case of Economic Policy Making in Britain." *Comparative Politics*, 25(3), 275–96.

Hjern, B. (1982). "Implementation Research—The Link Gone Missing." *Journal of Public Policy*, 2(3), 301–8.

Hjern, B. and Porter, D. O. (1993). "Implementation Structures: A New Unit of Administrative Analysis," in Hill, M. (Ed.), *The Policy Process: A Reader.* London: Harvester Wheatsheaf, pp. 248–65.

Hill, M. and Hupe, P. (2002). *Implementing Public Policy: Governance in Theory and Practice.* London: Sage Publications.

Hill, M. and Hupe, P. (2003). "The Multi-Layer Problem in Implementation Research." *Public Management Review*, 5(4), 471–90.

Hill, M. and Hupe, P. (2006). "Analysing Policy Processes as Multiple Governance: Accountability in Social Policy." *Policy & Politics*, 34(3), 557–73.

Hogwood, B. and Gunn, L. (1993). "Why 'Perfect Implementation' Is Unattainable." *The Policy Process. A Reader*, 2, 217–25.

Howlett, M. (2003). "Administrative Styles and the Limits of Administrative Reform: A Neo-Institutional Analysis of Administrative Culture." *Canadian Public Administration*, 46(4), 471–494.

Hupe, P. L. and Hill, M. J. (2015). "'And the Rest is Implementation'. Comparing Approaches to What Happens in Policy Processes beyond Great Expectations." *Public Policy and Administration*, 31(2), 103–21, doi:10.1177/09520767155 98828.

Knill, C. (1999). "Explaining Cross-National Variance in Administrative Reform: Autonomous versus Instrumental Bureaucracies." *Journal of Public Policy*, 19(2), 113–39.

Kotter, J. P. (1995). "Leading Change: Why Transformation Efforts Fail." *Harvard Business Review*, 85(1), 96.

Lindquist, E. (2006). "Organizing for Policy Implementation: The Emergence and Role of Implementation Units in Policy Design and Oversight." *Journal of Comparative Policy Analysis: Research and Practice*, 8(4), 311–24.

Lipsky, M. (1980). *Street-Level Bureaucracy: Dilemmas of the Individual in Public Services.* New York: Russell Sage Foundation.

Matland, R. E. (1995). "Synthesizing the Implementation Literature: The Ambiguity-Conflict Model of Policy Implementation." *Journal of Public Administration Research and Theory*, 5(2), 145–74.

May, P. J. (2003). "Policy Design and Implementation," in Peters, B. Guy and Pierre, Jon (Eds.), *Handbook of Public Administration.* Beverly Hills, CA: Sage, pp. 233–33.

O'Toole, L. J. (2000). "Research on Policy Implementation: Assessment and Prospects." *Journal of Public Administration Research and Theory*, 10(2), 263–88.

Patashnik, E. (2008). *Reforms at Risk: What Happens After Major Policy Changes Are Enacted.* Princeton, NJ: Princeton University Press.

Pressman, J. L. and Wildavsky, A. B. (1973). *Implementation: How Great Expectations in Washington are Dashed in Oakland*. Berkeley, CA: University of California Press.

Robichau, R. Waters and Lynn, L. E. (2009). "The Implementation of Public Policy: Still the Missing Links." *Policy Studies Journal*, 37(1), 21–36.

Rondinelli, D. A. (1983). *Development Projects as Policy Experiments: An Adaptive Approach to Development Administration*. London: Methuen.

Southard, M. (2016). "Implementing Challenging Policy and Systems Change: Identifying Leadership Competencies." *Human Service Organizations: Management, Leadership & Governance*, 40(1), 1–5.

Thomas, J. W. and M. S. Grindle (1990) "After the Decision: Implementing Policy Reforms in Developing Countries." *World Development*, 18(8), 1163–81.

Turner, M. and Hulme, D. (1997). *Governance, Administration and Development: Making the State Work*. Basingstoke: Macmillan.

Van Meter, D. and Van Horn, C.E. (1975). "The Policy Implementation Process: A Conceptual Framework." *Administration and Society*, 6(4), 445–88.

Werner, A. (2004). *A Guide to Implementation Research*. Washington DC: Urban Institute Press.

Williams, M. S. (2004). "Policy Component Analysis: A Method for Identifying Problems in Policy Implementation." *Journal of Social Service Research*, 30(4), 1–18.

Winter, S. (1990). "Integrating Implementation Research," in Palumbo, D. J. and Calisto, D. J. (Eds.), *Implementation and the Policy Process: Opening Up the Black Box*. New York: Greenwood Press, pp. 19–38.

6   Policy evaluation

Evaluation is a critical task in policy-making and occurs throughout the policy process as various actors assess policy issues, options, and program delivery modes. Many evaluation activities occur during *policy appraisal*, a term used to describe "*ex ante*" evaluation, before a policy or program is adopted. This is somewhat different from the kinds of evaluation described in this chapter, which are "*ex-post*"—happening *after* a policy has been implemented, with the aim of determining if and to what extent it has performed as expected. Although many of the techniques used in the two types of evaluation are similar—such as cost-benefit or cost-effectiveness evaluation (see Chapter 4)—their use after the fact is for a very different purpose, namely changing, altering, or terminating a policy based on how it actually performed up to the date of the evaluation, rather than attempting to predict its performance in the future.

The purpose of ex-post evaluation is ostensibly to feed into future iterations of policy-making in the form of learning or lesson-drawing from experience (as foreshadowed by Figure 5.1 in the last chapter). But it may also be conducted for many different purposes, including embarrassing opponents for (alleged) policy underperformance or failure. This reality of evaluation is at odds with the widespread perception that it is a technical activity intended for improving programs. It is often assumed, for example, that evaluation is simple, uniformly carried out, and reveals clear-cut and uncontested results that will drive policy reform. In reality, it is not a simple process in most cases, and is sometimes skipped entirely; and even when it is conducted, it often does not occur at a high level of sophistication (Hahn and Dudley 2004). Finally, the results of evaluations may be ignored or misinterpreted, so the expected learning experience does not occur.

Even when evaluation is conducted well, findings are often misinterpreted, misused, or contested by different actors depending on their interests and viewpoints. Government agencies and agencies, for example, have a strong vested interest in showing their policies have positive effects and are often convinced that their programs are effective and do not place much faith in formal evaluation.

The basics of policy evaluation

Policy evaluation refers broadly to all the activities carried out by a range of state and societal actors to determine how a policy has fared in practice and to estimate how it is likely to perform in the future. Evaluation examines both the means employed and the objectives served by a policy in practice. The results and recommendations from these evaluations are then fed back into further rounds of policy-making and can lead to the refinement of policy design and implementation or, infrequently, to its complete reform or termination.

After a policy has been put in place, how long should it remain? Especially if the aim of the policy was to cure or correct some issue and eliminate it either entirely or in great measure, when can it be safely scaled back or eliminated? And if it is unsuccessful, should it be reformed or terminated? And if it is to be reformed, how exactly should this be done? Or in the case of other programs which may persist for some time, is the government getting its money's worth? Budgets and personnel are not "fungible" but encounter opportunity costs. That is, money and time spent on one project are not easily transferred to another, but rather may prevent other new programs from going ahead. At what point should a government pull the plug on an existing program and opt for another?

Of course, decisions of this kind may be taken on purely ideological or other grounds, such as when one government nationalizes an industry only to see a successor government privatize it, or vice versa (Donahue 1989). However, in many cases governments and would like to see some evidence of policy success or failure, and the reasons for them, before deciding whether to continue, reform, or terminate a program. Evaluation can help them strengthen "value for money" arguments for these decisions, comply with fiscal accountability and auditing standards, negotiate budgets, and evaluate comparisons with other alternative projects. It can also help them improve policy/program design in the future, better understand the disparities between forecast and actual performance, and make their operations more efficient and better targeted.

But these same managers and actors must also keep in mind that the effects of policies are long term; they take time to emerge and become measurable. Such effects may also be very diffuse and too general to use particular indictors to measure what is being accomplished and that much of the real effect of a policy may not be quantifiable. A failure to identify the positive effects of a policy can be attributable both to the inadequacy of the evaluation and to the biases of the evaluator(s); policy actors need to guard against and prevent these from occurring. Specifically, evaluation contributes to the policy-making process by:

• synthesizing what is known about a problem and its proposed policy or program remedy;
• demystifying conventional wisdom related to either the problem or its solution(s);
• developing new information about program or policy effectiveness; and
• explaining to policy actors the implications of new information derived through evaluation.

But, like the activities found in most other stages of the policy process, policy evaluation is as much a political as a technical activity. The purpose is not always to reveal the effects of a policy but sometimes to disguise or conceal a situation that might, for example, show the government in poor light. It is also possible for public managers to design the terms of evaluation in such a way as to lead to preferred conclusions regarding the merits and demerits of particular policy options. Similarly, actors outside government may make policy evaluations with the intention of criticizing government actions in order to gain partisan political advantage or to reinforce their own ideological preferences for specific kinds of policy interventions.

Many different actors can be involved in policy evaluation. Each may have a different reason for conducting an evaluation and may do so in a unique way, using distinct methods and practices. These actors include *consultants* hired by governments to undertake technical analyses such as cost-benefit analysis; *legislatures and executives* who conduct wide-ranging inquiries in public or behind closed doors; *administrative agencies* which are often mandated to carry out periodic reviews of program; *the public*, who vote in elections at least in part retrospectively; and also *international actors and donors* who conduct project and program evaluations to ensure, among other things, that monies were well spent.

However, serious efforts in policy evaluation are rarely attempted by public managers for two primary reasons. First, negative evaluations may potentially harm a manager's reputation, resource base, or even career. Second, and at least as importantly, program evaluation is technically challenging, both in terms of the expertise required and also the data needed for its conduct. As a consequence, many ineffective or even harmful policies persist despite their less-than-optimal or even damaging consequences.

The process of policy evaluation

Defining the scope of evaluation

The scope of evaluation depends on the nature of the policy actors involved in its initiation and/or implementation, the amount of information available to them, and what they intend to do with the findings. Possible outcomes of this process range from maintenance of all aspects of an existing policy effort, changes in policy substance and process, to policy termination. Evaluation can involve merely assessment, through timely monitoring of how established programs are doing, or may address the deeper question of whether the assumptions underlining the policies are valid.

While some evaluative designs are more likely to produce credible estimates of policy outcomes than others, in practice it may be difficult or impossible to adopt the "best" evaluation design due to time and resource constraints. The evaluators should instead choose the best possible design by taking into consideration the importance of the policy, the practicality of evaluation designs, and the probability of producing useful and credible results. Wherever possible, efforts should be made to bolster the evaluation resources available both within government and also in the nongovernmental sector.

Determining evaluation criteria

Policy outcomes are often multifaceted, and different judgments can be made depending on which aspects of policy outcomes are emphasized. Evaluation criteria provide standards by which the policy outcomes can be evaluated. Evaluation criteria enable the evaluation to focus on the aspects of policy outcomes that are most important or most valued by those controlling the scope and design of the evaluation.

Evaluation criteria are often defined to correspond with the stated objectives of the policies. For example, the success of a policy designed to reduce school dropout rates is evaluated by the changes in school dropout rates before and after the implementation of the policy. While the use of evaluation criteria focusing on stated objectives of policies helps to promote the accountability of government agencies responsible for decision-making and implementation of these policies, it may also create a tendency to systematically dismiss other objectives that are interrelated with the stated objectives.

After evaluation criteria are defined, performance indicators should be selected to measure the criteria. Technical evaluation, especially, requires specific information on key measures—*benchmarks or performance indicators*—

that can be time-consuming or expensive to collect and analyze. The exact nature of the information required and the ability of evaluators to set indicators depends on the exact purpose and nature of the evaluation undertaken and varies according to the specific issues and concerns addressed by each program or policy. The design of measures requires careful thinking and testing in order to ensure that measures actually link performance to organizational goals. Errors in the construction of measures can easily lead to inappropriate behavioral and policy alterations that might further inhibit the attainment of policy goals rather than promote them. Measures must be reasonably reliable, valid, robust, and cost-effective. To guard against unintended consequences, multiple measures must be created that can be "triangulated" against each other to ensure that what is expected to be measured is actually what is being assessed.

Collecting information

There are two types of information collection methods that public managers should encourage so as to promote high-quality and useful evaluations: primary and secondary. Primary data are collected directly by the organization for the purpose of evaluation, while secondary data have been collected by outside organizations, typically for purposes other than the evaluation concerned. Examples of secondary data include national census data, financial market data, or demographic health survey data. Depending on the nature of the problem at hand, managers can demand more or less stringent or reliable sources of information, or focus on generating new information, or utilizing secondary sources. Each choice will have a significant impact on the policy evaluations that follow.

Evaluation can be based on existing data or require the creation of new data. Measures using existing data avoid additional costs associated with reporting and data collection, but may not measure as directly important individual and organizational behavior. Designing new measures based on new data, however, can be much more time-consuming and introduce the possibility of errors that could, in turn, lengthen the time and expense required to generate significant results.

Conducting evaluation

Once evaluation criteria have been defined and the relevant information collected, there is the all-important task of analyzing the information and drawing conclusions from the analysis. What information and analytical technique is selected and how and when they are analyzed depends on the type of evaluation being sought, which is discussed in the following section.

Types of evaluation

Policy evaluation concentrates on one or more of the following types of information about policies' performance: Input, Process, Output, Outcome, or Impact, as depicted in Figure 6.1 below.

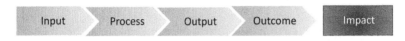

Figure 6.1 Types of evaluation

The choice of performance indicators affects how it is analyzed, the level of analytical difficulty, and the scope of the conclusions. Generally speaking, "Input" evaluation is the simplest form of evaluation, requiring simple information and analytical tools while the opposite is true for "Impact" evaluation. While impact evaluation should be preferred when searching for a comprehensive understanding of all the policy's costs, activities, and effects, the requirements for conducting it may be too high to be realistically done on a routine basis. The different and progressively difficult demands of different types of policy evaluation are illustrated in the following diagram depicting evaluation of a hypothetical handwashing public campaign.

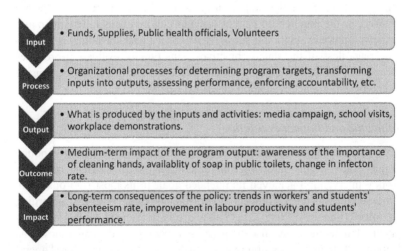

Figure 6.2 Handwashing campaign: types of evaluation

Simple evaluations

Input evaluation

The focus of such evaluation is to measure the quantity of program inputs, that is, the amount of effort governments put into accomplishing their goals. The input may be personnel, office space, communication, transportation, and so on—all of which are calculated in terms of the monetary costs they involve. The purpose of the evaluation is often to establish a baseline of data that can be used for further evaluations of efficiency or quality of service delivery.

Process evaluation

The focus is to examine the organizational processes—including rules and operating procedures—and activities undertaken to deliver programs. The objective of recording the information on the delivery process is to assess if it can be streamlined and made more efficient. Towards this objective, implementation of a policy is usually broken down into discrete tasks, such as strategic planning, financial management, and client relations, and then one or more of these tasks are examined to see if they can be improved.

Output evaluation

The focus of such evaluation is to examine program outputs rather than inputs. Examples of the outputs may be hospital beds or school places created, or the numbers of patients seen or children taught. The main aim of performance evaluation is simply to determine what the policy is producing, regardless of the stated objectives. This type of evaluation produces benchmark or performance data that are used for more comprehensive outcome and impact evaluation described below.

Outcome and impact evaluation

The crux of program evaluation involves the design of measures of policy inputs and outputs allowing the determination of whether or not a policy intervention achieved its intended goal. In its most rigorous form, "measurement is the assignment of numerals to objects or events according to rules" (Langbein 2006: 21). This extends not simply to the measurement of outcomes, but also to processes leading to the outcomes. The conduct of impact evaluation requires that (1) the policy goals are "operationalizable"; (2) appropriate indicators can be designed and implemented that allow observation of progress towards goal achievement; and (3) appropriate data exists to allow the measures to be calculated and comparisons made.

Evaluators should distinguish between gross outcomes and net outcomes of a policy (McLaughlin, 1985). Gross outcomes consist of all observed changes in an outcome measure for the policy, and net outcomes are those effects that can be directly attributed to the policy. At any given time, the effects of a particular policy are closely intertwined with the effects of other policies and events, and thus the observed policy impacts are often the combination of the effects of a particular policy together with many other factors. Therefore, the central task of technical policy evaluation is frequently to isolate the effects of a particular policy from those caused by other factors, as depicted in Figure 6.3.

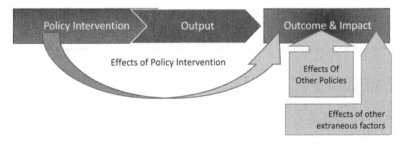

Figure 6.3 Central task of policy evaluation: netting out policy effects from other factors

Source: adapted from Rossi, Lipsey, and Freeman, 2004.

The relationship between gross outcomes and net outcomes can be expressed as: Gross outcome = {net outcome} + {effects of other policies} + {effects of other events}. The effects of other policies and events also include cumulative effects, which may be difficult to attribute to any single set of causes.

Table 6.1 lists three commonly used evaluation designs in isolating the net outcome from gross outcome. While some designs are more likely to produce more credible estimates of policy outcomes than others, in practice it is often difficult or impossible to adopt the "best" evaluation design due to time and resource constraints. The evaluators should instead choose the best possible design by taking into consideration the importance of the policy, the practicality of evaluation designs, and the probability of producing useful and credible results.

Table 6.1 Evaluation design for isolating net outcomes from gross outcomes

Type	Description
1. Randomized controlled trials	A randomized controlled trial establishes the net impact of a policy by exposing a group of people to the policy intervention in question (the experimental group) while withholding the policy to a comparison group (the control group). The allocation of people or units to the experimental and control group is undertaken on a randomized basis.
2. Simple before/after comparison	A single sample of the population is selected and are exposed to a policy or program initiative, and the net effect size is measured in terms of the difference in the outcome of interest before and after the intervention is introduced.
3. Matched comparison	In this design, an experimental group is exposed to a policy whilst a closely matched control group does not receive the policy in question.

Utilization of evaluation results

Policy learning

One of the primary purposes of evaluation is, or at least should be, policy learning whereby policy actors learn about what works and why. Ideally, the resulting learning will subsequently form the basis for further improvement in programs. There are four types of learning that occur in the policy arena: *social learning, policy-oriented learning, lesson-drawing*, and *government learning*. These four types differ in terms of what is learned and where the lessons arise.

Social learning (Hall 1993) is the most general and significant type of learning that policy managers can promote and to which they must react. It involves fundamental shifts in public attitudes and perceptions of social problems and policy issues and involves many different types of actors, both inside and outside of governments and existing policy subsystems.

Lesson-drawing is a more limited, means-oriented, type of learning (Rose 1991). It involves a variety of actors inside of existing subsystems, who draw lessons from their own experiences and the experiences of others in implementing existing policies. It is significant at the stage of policy formulation and can also appear in carefully designed evaluative efforts if these provide positive or negative exemplars that evaluators can use as benchmarks for evaluative activities.

Policy-oriented learning is a type of learning that occurs largely within existing policy communities and involves the clarification of existing goals and policy beliefs based on experiences gained from evaluations of existing policies (Sabatier 1987). It is the most common type of learning to emerge from typical policy evaluation activities. In Sabatier's view (1987: 150–151), policy-oriented learning generally involves: (1) improving one's understanding of the state of variables defined as important by one's belief system (or, secondarily, by competing belief systems); (2) refining one's understanding of logical and causal relationships internal to a belief system; and (3) identifying and responding to challenges to one's belief system. Thus, as Sabatier puts it: "policy-oriented learning . . . is an ongoing process of search and adaptation motivated by the desire to realize core policy beliefs" (p. 151). Ultimately, then, what is learned is how to better achieve one's ends or how to better implement public policies.

Government learning is the most restricted type of learning (Etheredge 1981). It involves reviews of policy and program behavior by existing actors and tends to be means-oriented at best. Its impact and consequences are generally limited to improvement of the means by which policies are implemented and administered.

Policy termination

Unlike proposals for reform or simply the continuation of the status quo arising from policy evaluation, the option of *policy termination* suggests a complete cessation of the policy in question (de Leon 1983). Like more limited proposals for reform, consideration of this option involves the incorporation of the results of an evaluative process, back into the policy process, usually directly to the decision-making stage. However, although it is fairly common for evaluations, especially politically motivated ones, to suggest the adoption of a termination option, policymakers are typically reluctant to take on this course of action. This is partially due to the inherent difficulties of arriving at an agreement on whether the policy was a success or failure. But it is also typical for existing programs and policies to have established beneficiaries and, often, to have become institutionalized to such an extent that their cessation is a costly process involving considerable legal, bureaucratic, and political expense. Accounts of such events usually underscore the extent to which termination often requires an ideological shift in government and society allowing uniform judgments of success or failure to be made (Jordan et al. 2013).

It should also be mentioned that a successful termination in the short term does not guarantee a similar long-term result. That is, if the perception of a problem persists, the termination decision itself will feed back into reconceptualization of problems and policy choices. If no other suitable alternative emerges, this can result in the reinstatement of a terminated program or policy, or the adoption and implementation of a close equivalent.

Challenges in policy evaluation

Similar to other activities in the policy process, there are technical, political, and operational challenges to conduct of policy evaluations. The policy evaluation functions outlined above require either a highly trained workforce with future-oriented management and excellent information base and data-processing capacities, or the ability to effectively outsource policy research to outside experts. They also require sufficient coordination among participating organizations to ensure that the research being undertaken is relevant and timely. However, these conditions are rarely satisfied, by even otherwise capable governments.

Serious efforts in policy evaluation are hampered by the following technical and organizational constraints:

1. *Lack of organizational support.* There is often no administrative mandate for evaluation activities, and neither dedicated agencies nor sufficient resources are made available to carry out evaluation even if it is required for major policy decisions.
2. *Shortage of evaluation skills.* In most developing countries and many developed countries, evaluation departments are staffed by civil servants without training and experience in evaluation. Worse still, because of the low priority often given to evaluation, those assigned to evaluation tasks are often regarded as side-tracked from promotion to more operations-oriented departments, further undermining the legitimacy of evaluators and evaluation.
3. *Narrow perception of the scope of evaluation.* Much of the evaluation effort in many government agencies has been directed to input- and perhaps output-based evaluation intended to keep track of implementation of the policy. Such evaluations are essentially bookkeeping in nature and yield limited insights into the program's performance.
4. *Insufficient capacity for data collection.* Although this shortcoming is not restricted to policy evaluation, the strenuous data requirements of evaluation make this problem a binding and severe constraint. For example, the baseline data essential for any serious evaluation are often not collected before new policies are introduced, and there are few remedial measures that can be taken for this lack once policies are implemented.

The above technical and organizational constraints are closely intertwined with a set of political considerations, further diminishing the opportunities for thorough and meaningful policy evaluation:

1. *Politically charged environment for policy evaluation.* The findings of policy evaluation may have significant implications for elections and/or allocations of resources among different stakeholders. Some actors may also wish to disguise or suppress evidence regarding the results of policy initiatives, thereby avoiding blame for a failure or claiming credit for a "success" in misleading ways. A government may be so closely associated with a particular policy that it might ignore contrary evidence of its effectiveness. As a result, developing adequate and acceptable methods for policy evaluation and "evaluating evaluation" itself are difficult and contentious tasks.

2. *Unclear goals and subjectivity in interpreting results.* Goals in public policy are often not stated clearly enough to find out if, and to what extent, they are achieved. In fact, policy goals generated through the political system are often kept deliberately vague in order to secure enough political support for their passage.

3. *The subjective nature of the interpretation of evaluation findings.* Performance of a policy is neither so simple nor so certain as many contemporary critics of policy and politics would suggest. Success and failure are highly subjective concepts and the same condition can be interpreted very differently by different evaluators, often with no definitive way of determining who is right. Which interpretation prevails is often ultimately determined by political conflicts and compromises among the various actors.

4. *Self-interest.* The desire on the part of policy actors to use evaluation to enhance policy effectiveness may be constrained by their career aspirations and concerns for their future. Unfavorable evaluation of programs may potentially lead to a restriction of their opportunities for promotion.

Strategies for evaluators

Policy actors can take several steps to help overcome the barriers to evaluation that they face.

Clarifying evaluation criteria, benchmarking, and performance measures

One method involves defining clear evaluation criteria at the time of designing the program so that evaluators can better focus on the most salient aspects of policy outcomes. Policy outcomes are often multifaceted and different judgments can be made depending on which aspects of policy outcomes are emphasized. The extent to which the evaluation criteria are set in advance mitigates opportunities for misunderstanding or gaming.

However, while focusing on stated objectives helps to hold relevant agencies accountable, it may also lead to the neglect of other objectives. To ensure against a narrow evaluation scope, the inclusion of broader criteria may be appropriate. For example, a policy designed to reduce school dropout rates can also be evaluated on its impact on important economic and social development dimensions.

"Benchmarking" is a key method of determining the appropriate level of policy performance. It is the process of comparing internal performance measures and results against those of others involved in similar activities. It is shorthand for a process of surveying other similar organizations and programs in order to assess "best practices" and the standards to use in comparing and assessing the performance of the agency or policy being evaluated. It involves a systematic effort to compare one's own practices and outputs against others.

The information needs of different policy evaluation techniques and the criteria used for monitoring policy progress and forming judgments about policy success and failure vary according to the specific type of analysis required. In most cases, however, policy evaluation requires the establishment of information systems and analytical units in order to allow benchmarking criteria to be developed and to continually assess changes in policy results on the ground.

Establishing independent evaluation departments within government agencies

Policy actors should understand the political nature of much evaluation but should also strive to enhance its technical quality. Technical sophistication will not only give them leverage but also enhance the quality of policymaking, helping policymakers and programs to achieve better long-term results. They can, for example, set up monitoring and evaluation frameworks before policy implementation begins, building mechanisms to ensure independence in the evaluation (internal versus external evaluators), and better link monitoring efforts with impact assessment. They can also broaden channels for the communication of evaluation outcomes to main stakeholders.

One way this can be done is by establishing or promoting the establishment of arm's-length or quasi-independent evaluation units or agencies. Such agencies can be established either within an existing agency or as an outside auditor. Internal evaluators have certain strengths, such as easier access to the data and a better understanding of policy/ program aims and experiences;

but they may be biased. External agencies, on the other hand, enjoy the reverse situation: access to data can be problematic, but independence of judgment is enhanced.

Strengthening nongovernmental participation

Lack of "boundary-spanning" links between governmental and nongovernmental organizations is often a critical problem in public sector evaluations. Policymakers should therefore nurture a healthy policy research community outside government because of its potential to enrich public understanding of policy issues and support the policy analytical capacity of the government.

Consultation with affected stakeholders is as vital to policy evaluation as it is to other policy activities. There are many mechanisms for such consultations that public managers conducting evaluation might potentially embrace. These include setting up administrative forums for public hearings and establishing special consultative committees, task forces, and inquiries for evaluative purposes. These can range, at the extremes, from small meetings of less than a dozen participants lasting several minutes to multimillion-dollar inquiries that hear thousands of individual briefs and can take years to complete. In many polities, political evaluation of government action is built into the system in the form of congressional or parliamentary overview committees or mandated administrative review processes. While in some countries, such as the US, the UK, Australia, and New Zealand, these tend to occur on a regular basis, in others the process may be less routine, as political reviews are undertaken on a more ad hoc basis.

Participatory monitoring and evaluation (PME) is a useful technique for evaluating policies (see German and Gohl 1996). PME is a process through which stakeholders at various levels:

- engage in monitoring or evaluating a particular project, program, or policy;
- share control over the content, the process, and the results of the activity; and
- engage in identifying and taking corrective actions.

PME is based on the assumption that it is stakeholders themselves who best know how a program is performing on the ground and how and to what extent it can be improved in practical terms. Actively engaging with them and supporting them with timely and relevant information is therefore an effective way to promote meaningful evaluation. Table 6.2 illustrates the differences between conventional and participatory types of analysis.

Table 6.2 Conventional and participatory modes of evaluation

	Conventional	Participatory
Who plans and manages the process	Project managers, outside experts	Local people, project managers and staff, other stakeholders
Role of primary stakeholders	Provide information only	Collect and analyze information, share findings, take actions
How success is measured	Externally defined, mainly quantitative indicators	Internally defined indicators, more qualitative indicator
Approach	Predetermined, follows standard format	Adapts as necessary, based on purpose and information available

Source: adapted from Institute of Development Studies, 1998.

The greatest danger of PME is the possibility of "group think" and even nepotism whereby stakeholders collude to generate upbeat evaluations. Mechanisms promoting critical inquiry and robust debates should be able to guard against these potential barriers to PME.

Conclusion: focusing on learning

Evaluation is a key policy function to which policy actors should devote more care and attention than they commonly do. The technical, operational, and political barriers to effective evaluation are no doubt steep but so are the rewards of overcoming them. Having said that, one must not underestimate the difficulties, especially for outcome and impact evaluation which are being increasingly demanded by policymakers and donor agencies. There is simply not enough information, analytical skills, organizational and political support, and time available for a thorough evaluation of outcomes, much less overall impact. More often than not, however, agencies will derive plentiful benefits from process evaluation connecting inputs to outputs. Participatory monitoring and evaluation of routine performance data especially offers vast potential for assessing performance and drawing practical policy conclusions.

Rather than shy away from participation in the evaluation process, public managers should engage fully in it. Such engagement extends to the use of foresight to design evaluation right into the heart of the policy itself. With their longevity, experience, and ability to participate in policy-making from agenda-setting right through to evaluation and beyond, public managers are in an ideal position to ensure that the policy process is one that features as much learning and improvement as possible.

References

Bennett, C. J. and Howlett, M. (1992). "The Lessons of Learning: Reconciling Theories of Policy Learning and Policy Change." *Policy Sciences*, 25(3), 275–94.

Bernstein, S. and Cashore, B. (2012). "Complex Global Governance and Domestic Policies: Four Pathways of Influence." *International Affairs*, 88(3), 585–604.

Chelimsky, E. (1995). "New Dimensions in Evaluation," in *Evaluation and Development: Proceedings of the World Bank Conference on Evaluation and Development*, edited by World Bank, International Bank for Reconstruction and Development, Washington DC: The World Bank, pp. 3–14.

Cohen, W. M. and Levinthal, D. A. (1990). "Absorptive Capacity: A New Perspective on Learning and Innovation." *Administrative Science Quarterly*, 35, 128–52.

Davidson, E. J. (2005). *Evaluation Methodology Basics*. Thousand Oaks, CA: Sage.

DeLeon, P. (1983). "Policy Evaluation and Program Termination." *Policy Studies Review*, 2(4), 631–47.

Donahue, J. D. (1989). *The Privatization Decision: Public Ends, Private Means.* New York: Basic Books.

Etheredge, L. S. (1981). "Government Learning: An Overview," in Long, S. L. (Ed.), *The Handbook of Political Behaviour*. New York: Plenum.

German, D. and Gohl, E. (Eds.), (1996). Participatory Impact Monitoring Booklet 4: The concept of participatory impact monitoring. Eschborn: GATE/GTZ. www.sswm.info/sites/default/files/reference_attachments/GERMAN%20and%20GOHL%201996%20PIM%20Booklet%204%20The%20Concept%20of%20Participatory%20Impact%20Monitoring.pdf

Hahn, R. W. and Dudley, P. (July 2007). "How Well Does the Government Do Cost-Benefit Analysis." *Review of Environmental Economics and Policy*, 1(2), 197–211. doi:10.1093/reep/rem012. .

Hall, P. (1993). "Policy Paradigms, Social Learning and the State: The Case of Economic Policy-Making in Britain." *Comparative Politics*, 25(3), 275–96.

Hovi, J., Sprinz, F. F., and Underdal, A. (2003). "The Oslo-Potsdam Solution to Measuring Regime Effectiveness: Critique, Response, and the Road Ahead." *Global Environmental Policy*, 3(3), 74–96.

Institute of Development Studies (1998). Participatory Monitoring and Evaluation. IDS Policy Briefing, Issue 12. Available online at www.ids.ac.uk/files/dmfile/PB12.pdf.

Jordan, A., Bauer, M. W., and Green-Pedersen, C. (2013). "Policy Dismantling." *Journal of European Public Policy*, 20(5), 795–805. doi:10.1080/13501763.2013.771092.

Langbein, L. and Felbinger, C. L. (2006). *Public Program Evaluation: A Statistical Guide*. Armonk, NY: M.E. Sharpe.

May, P. J. (1992). "Policy Learning and Failure." *Journal of Public Policy*, 12(4), 331–54.

McLaughlin, M. W. (1985). "Implementation Realities and Evaluation Design," in Shotland, R. L. and Mark, M. M. (Eds.), *Implementation Realities and*

Evaluation Design. Social Science and Social Policy. Beverly Hills, CA: SAGE, pp. 96–120. Later published in Rossi and Freeman (1993).

Mitchell, R. and Nicholas, S. (2006). "Knowledge Creation Through Boundary Spanning." *Knowledge Management Research and Practice*, 4, 310–18.

Mohan, R., Bernstein, D. J., and Whitsett, M. D. (Eds.), (2002). *Responding to Sponsors and Stakeholders in Complex Evaluation Environments, Vol. 95.* San Francisco, CA: Jossey-Bass.

Palumbo, D. J. (1987). *The Politics of Program Evaluation.* Beverly Hills, CA: Sage.

Roche, C. (1999). Impact Assessment for Development Agencies: Learning to value change, Oxfam GB, http://policy-practice.oxfam.org.uk/publications/impact-assessment-for-development-agencies-learning-to-value-change-122808

Rose, R. (1991). "What is Lesson-Drawing." *Journal of Public Policy*, 11(1), 3–30.

Rossi, P. H., Lipsey, M. W., and Freeman, H. E. (2004). *Evaluation: A Systematic Approach.* Thousand Oaks, CA: Sage.

Sabatier, P. (1987). "Knowledge, Policy-Oriented Learning, and Policy Change: An Advocacy Coalition Framework." *Science Communication*, 8(4), 649–92.

Sanderson, I. (2002). "Evaluation, Policy Learning and Evidence-Based Policy Making." *Public Administration*, 80(1), 1–22.

Stufflebeam, D. L. (2001). "Evaluation Models." *New Directions for Evaluation*, 89, 7–98.

Swiss, J. E. (1991). *Public Management Systems: Monitoring and Managing Government Performance.* Upper Saddle River, NJ: Prentice Hall.

Triantafillou, P. (2007). "Benchmarking in the Public Sector: A Critical Conceptual Framework." *Public Administration*, 85(3), 829–46.

Weber, E. P. and Khademian, A. M. (2008). "Wicked Problems, Knowledge Challenges and Collaborative Capacity Builders in Network Settings." *Public Administration Review*, 68(2), 334–49.

Young, O. (1991). "Political Leadership and Regime Formation in International Society." *International Organization*, 45(3), 281–308.

7 Conclusion

Influencing the policy process

Public dissatisfaction with their governments is strong the world over, as is evident in the success of politicians who present themselves as "outsiders" or "anti-establishment" in elections in many countries in the developed and developing worlds. Much of the cynicism and disaffection is rooted in the populations' deep frustration with undesirable conditions they face in their social and economic lives. Another large part of the blame for the situation rests with the politicians' inability to meet their stated goals, which is viewed by the population as the result of deliberate efforts to deceive voters with promises they had no intention of keeping. The reality may be more prosaic: it is possible that in many contexts, neither politicians nor their supporting staff understand the multidimensional problems faced by societies, or the solutions to them. The shortcoming is aggravated by the many lapses that occur during the course of implementing a policy. If true, inability and misunderstanding rather than ill-intent lies at the source of the problem.

The limitations of governmental and nongovernmental officials engaged in the policy process are shared by scholars of public policy, who often espouse a view of the field that is idealistic at best and often impossible to achieve in practice. In this view, all that policymakers need to do is set an objective and find the most efficient, equitable, and acceptable means of achieving it. The purpose of this book has been to highlight the many challenges that policymakers face—anticipating and defining problems; discovering, assessing, and selecting solutions; implementing their chosen solution, and evaluating performance—and to offer suggestions on how the challenges may be overcome. The key challenges and suggested strategic responses are summarized in Table 7.1.

Responding to the challenges adequately requires a range of skills and resources, which brings us to squarely face the issue of capacity of governments to make and implement policies.

Table 7.1   Summary: policy process and the associated policy challenges and responses

Policy process	Challenges	Response strategy
Agenda-setting	Governments not knowing what they want to do or should do, or seeking unattainable agendas	Place only significant policy problems onto the government's policy agenda; examine existing and potential agenda items within an integrated framework that takes related goals into account
Policy formulation	Attempting to deal with complex problems without appropriately investigating problem causes or the probable effects of policy alternatives	Develop a range of policy options that may potentially address the targeted issues in a way that is consistent with the basic policy goals
Decision-making	Failing to anticipate adverse and other policy consequences or risk of system failures	Select options that promote integrated policy goals and are acceptable to a broad range of stakeholders
Policy implementation	Failing to deal with implementation problems including lack of legitimacy, principle-agent problems, etc.	Translate adopted policies into action through appropriate mix of direction and incentives, taking integrated goals into account
Policy evaluation	Lack of learning due to inadequate or inappropriate monitoring and/or feedback processes	Review the implementation of the adopted policies against set criteria that reflect integrated policy goals

Source: Adapted from Howlett, 2009b

The key role of policy capacity

The problems and challenges in policy-making and implementation noted above can be overcome, but only through concerted and protracted efforts. Making the right policy choices and implementing them well are good aspirations, but ultimately meaningless if the policy actors lack the skills and resources to do this. Are governments and their civil society partners actually equipped to manage the policy process in the manner proposed in this book? Do they have what it takes to perform vital functions in making, implementing, and evaluating policies?

Policymakers and scholars have recognized the importance of policy capacity for some decades now. Indeed, international donor agencies have directed as much as a quarter of all international aid—hundreds of billions of dollars over the years—to what they call technical assistance, institutional reform, or simply capacity-building. The growing popularity of professional training in public policy and public administration is inspired by a similar urge to improve policies. Concerns about capacity gaps have sparked a similar interest among scholars about the nature of policy capacity, its definition and composition (Fukuyama 2013; Savoia and Sen 2014; OECD 2006).

Policy capacity involves analytical capabilities, such as enhancing "the ability of governments to make intelligent choices" (Painter and Pierre 2005), to scan the environment and set strategic directions (Howlett and Lindquist 2004; Savoie 2003), to weigh and assess the implications of policy alternatives (Bakvis 2000), and to make appropriate use of knowledge in policy-making (Parsons 2004; Peters 1996). Others include additional skills and resources such as acquisition and utilization of policy-relevant knowledge, the ability to frame options, the application of both qualitative and quantitative research methods to policy problems, the effective use of communications, and stakeholder management strategies (Howlett 2009a; Oliphant and Howlett 2010). But other key capacity areas also exist in the kinds of operational and political resources available to governments and other actors, not only at the individual level but also at the organizational and systemic ones.

The nine components of capacity are set out in Table 7.2. Each of the nine cells formed by the first two columns represents a specific bundle of skills and resources required to carry out policy functions.

It is not necessary for all elements in a governance system to possess all the nine sets of skills and resources all the time; some sectors and functions may place higher demand on some and not others. Ministries of finance, for example, may need more analytical skills than most other agencies, but even they would require at least a modicum of other skills. Similarly, ministries of health would require more skills in health policy and management while cultural ministries may require more skills in community engagement. What particular skills and resources an agency or policy actor requires cannot be specified in the abstract, but rather must be based on specific policy goals and estimated by the relevant individuals and agencies themselves.

Analytical skills and resources

Building and utilizing analytical skills for diagnosing problems, assessing solutions, and planning and evaluating implementation are vital for the success of policy efforts. Modern information technology has greatly reduced

Table 7.2 Policy capacity: skills and resources

Skills	Resources	Capacity component	Score 0–2 (see p. 148)
Analytical	Individual	Domain knowledge General research skills Skills in policy analysis	
	Organizational	Availability of individuals with analytical skills Processes for collecting and analyzing data Organizational commitment to evidence-based policy	
	Systemic	Access to policy consultants Political support for rigorous policy analysis Allowing access to organizational data and information	
Operational	Individual	Visionary leadership Results orientation and conflict management skills Strategic and operational management skills	
	Organizational	Availability of financial and human resources and management system Coordination of internal processes System for monitoring agency performance	
	Systemic	Intergovernmental and interagency coordination Coherence of relevant societal groups Rule of law, impartiality and corruption control	
Political	Individual	Networking skills Interpersonal influence Communicative capacity	
	Organizational	Organizational legitimacy (external) Access to key policymakers Process for public engagement	
	Systemic	Political Accountability for Policies Public trust in government Participation of civil society (e.g. NGOs) in the policy process	

Source: Adapted from Wu, Ramesh, and Howlett, 2015.

the costs of collecting and disseminating information, but it has not always been accompanied by an enhanced capability to use the information. As a result, policies often continue to be made without a sufficient understanding of causes of the problems and the solutions available to address them. This is true not only for "wicked" problems, such as income inequality and climate change, but also for more routine issues as traffic congestion and the quality of schools and hospitals. Lack of analytical skills in government creates a bias toward maintaining the status quo or for measures that do not require sophisticated analysis. When the problem becomes intolerable due to inaction or misguided action, policymakers without such capacity resort to ill-considered, "bold" moves with dubious prospects for success.

The analytical skills necessary for performing policy functions include knowledge of the relevant policy domain, general research skills in social sciences, and skills in conducting applied policy analysis. Scientific expertise is important both to disseminate potential solutions directly to policymakers and in its contribution to agenda-setting (Edwards 1999). There is no escape from the need for policy analysts (and distributed teams of policy analysts) to possess a substantive knowledge of a policy sector along with a strong understanding of the realities of public service delivery (Radin 2013). Thus, for example, an agency in charge of health care requires skills as diverse as health economics, primary health, hospital management, actuarial sciences, demography, and statistics and so on, in addition to medicine and general management. In reality, many departments of health around the world are staffed largely by generalist officers drawn from the broader civil service with no particular skills or training in health policy. When such a situation exists, the concerned agency is not only unable to understand the problems afflicting the sector, but must depend on the self-serving advice it receives from the industry. Systematic domain knowledge is critical, as it guides more prudent policy judgment and can play a mediative role in resolving controversies and achieving mutual consensus on policy problems (Renn 1995).

Agencies also need to set up processes for routine collection and the dissemination of monitoring data. Without the availability of sufficient data and convenient access to it, even the best-trained analysts are unlikely to understand the nature and extent of a problem, much less how to address it or to evaluate efforts to correct it. While the problem of reliable and compre-hensive data on policy issues exists in all countries, it is especially acute in developing countries, where statistical agencies are typically under-funded and insufficiently staffed relative to the vast developmental challenges they face.

Organizational commitment to evidence-based policy-making and imple-mentation can be furthered by the presence of a dedicated unit for conducting policy research and generating policy advice. Explicit organizational policies and procedures for conducting and utilizing cost-benefit analysis and impact evaluation studies stimulate the process of continuous policy learning (Radaelli 2009).

Maintaining a robust e-government architecture, for example, is increasingly recognized as vital for operational capability as it allows officials to connect and collaborate more easily and frequently and connects governments to people by facilitating popular input into designing programs and delivering public services (Moon et al. 2014; Akeroyd 2009). Internally, information technology offers potential for improving integration and coordination within the public sector while enhancing the use of analytical skills (Ambali 2010).

At the system level, a robust national information system for policy development allows gathering and sharing of information more quickly among all stakeholders and the general public than could be done at individual level. The architecture for collecting and disseminating information within and across public sector agencies and the society at large through, for example, national statistical agencies and periodic censuses is a major determinant of policy performance of individuals and agencies. Such a system provides for re-use of existing information without duplication of efforts through agency libraries, databases, and websites.

Operational skills and resources

Operational skills are relevant not only to policy implementation, as commonly believed, but to all policy functions. Policy leaders have long been recognized for the role they play in getting things done (Wallis and Dollery 1999; Morgan and Watson 1992; Zhang and Feiock 2010). Leadership involves management of organizations and enabling staff to lead themselves and creating a partnership with other agencies (British Cabinet Office 2001). Policy entrepreneurs estimate and mobilize the necessary resources for their specific "policy quests" (Wallis and Dollery 1997; Galanti 2014). Negotiation and conflict management skills of officials are also of vital importance for the smooth functioning of organizations. A high level of interpersonal skills is similarly important because the complexity of contemporary policy challenges requires close collaboration among a large number of policy professionals within and across organizations. Policy managers adept at negotiation and conflict management are better able to manage network governance and policy coordination towards coherence and the attainment of common goals (Klijn and Koppenjan 2000; Peters 1998).

Operational competences at the organizational level center on the effectiveness of organizations in mobilizing and deploying the resources necessary to carry out policy tasks. The traditional bureaucracy based on command and control, with roots in military practices, faces severe challenges in the context of democratic governments dealing with myriad and complex policy problems requiring high levels of coordination as well as transparency and participation. Meeting these challenges requires carefully designed organizational processes and practices within and across agencies, which are difficult to establish for a variety of reasons. Functional specialization by policy sector (e.g. education, health, defense), tasks (e.g. accounting, legal affairs), and geography (e.g. national and regional offices) within and across agencies make coordination difficult. The spread of various forms of decentralization, which transfers enhanced authority to local governments, has accentuated the challenge. Nepotism and corruption compound a general lack of financial and personnel resources to systematically undermine the organizational capacity of public organizations in some settings.

At the system level, operational capacity refers to public sector agencies' relationships with external governmental and nongovernmental partners. First, operational capacity is determined by the level of intergovernmental (e.g. federal, provincial, local) and interagency coordination. While the formal responsibility for addressing particular problems may continue to reside in particular agencies, most contemporary problems cut across agencies, sectors, and levels of government and make external coordination a vital necessity. All public organizations recognize this need, but few succeed in establishing appropriate institutions, processes, and practices for addressing it. The commonly used inter-departmental and intergovernmental meetings are episodic and ritualistic, and do not offer the continuing, substantive coordination that is needed.

Second, the coherence and active engagement of the relevant policy networks and communities in the policy process is also a key to operational capazcity. There is a substantial literature arguing that addressing complex public problems increasingly requires public agencies to partner and collaborate with their counterparts in the civil society; those with strong links make better choices, and implement policies better (Salamon 2002). Large and conflict-ridden policy communities tend to undermine rather than promote effective policies.

Political skills and resources

Finally, political skills and resources are vital because policies need to attract both legitimacy and resources from their authorizing institutions and constituencies to be effective. Proactive political engagement with stakeholders, and the management of vital relationships, are essential for generating the political support needed to implement and improve policies. This requires a sufficient number of politically skilled public managers, working in the context of supportive set of political institutions and processes. Political skills and resources may be the hardest capacity component to specify and build, but they have the capacity to shape or undermine other capacities.

Applying the capacity framework

The framework for policy capacity—comprising political, operational, and analytical skills at individual, organizational, and systemic levels—presented here is intended to allow policy organizations to assess their readiness for managing the policy process as outlined in this book. Viewing policy capacity as a bundle of nine capacity components allows for a clearer and more comprehensive understanding of the concept. It also offers practical tools to policymakers for assessing their own policy capacity and devising ways to build it. Of course, not all policy skills are equally valuable in a given context, and understanding how they are nested within each other is a critical concern for understanding identifying and rectifying capacity gaps. Specific needs and mitigation strategies will vary widely across policy sectors and agencies, and should be adjusted based on collective reflection and deliberation within agencies.

We may return to Table 7.2 (p. 144), and reinterpret it as a format for a simple scorecard for the summary self-assessment of an agency's policy capacity. Each indicator can be rated using a scale of 0–2, with 0 as "Build from scratch," 1 as "Could do better," and 2 as "No further effort required." The adjectival ratings symbolize the level of action required to improve a specific aspect of policy capacity. It does not seek to definitively measure an agency's policy capacity, but rather provides guidance on which dimension of policy capacity may require more immediate remedial efforts.

Conclusion: overcoming barriers to integrated public policy

This book has laid out several strategies that can be pursued for addressing the challenges of integrated and effective policy-making. The joint consideration of all key policy goals—economic, social, and environmental, at the very least—should be a mandatory requirement if policy-making is to overcome problems stemming from its typically segmented, sectoral nature. Simultaneous consideration of all three vital goals enables a fuller understanding of the policy challenges faced by society and how to achieve them. And a longer-term time horizon needs to be adopted to allow fuller consideration of environmental and social consequences along with economic effects. Taking a long-term view casts both problems and their solutions in a very different light, and opens up new opportunities for envisioning policy trade-offs, since addressing the estimation of costs and benefits can be spread over a much longer period of time.

Notwithstanding substantial barriers, improving integration throughout the policy-making process in the fashion set out in this book is a goal worth striving for. Better agenda management, improved analytical capacity, evidence-based decision-making, and working with policy communities are critical. Where barriers to integrated policy-making are greatest, for instance in "weak state" settings, welfare gains flowing from even marginal improvements to policy-making effectiveness may often be the greatest. Efforts in this direction, even where partially successful, support learning over time, and this learning is the only way to provide a foundation for future gains. Public managers should dedicate themselves to this task.

References

ADB. (2011). *Practical Guide to Capacity Development in a Sector Context.* Mandaluyong: Asian Development Bank.

Akeroyd, J. (2009). "Information Architecture and e-government." *INFuture,* 687–701. www.infoz.ffzg.hr/INFuture/2009/papers%5CINFuture2009.pdf .

Ambali, A.R. (2010). "E-government in Public Sector: Policy Implications and Recommendations for Policy-makers." *Research Journal of International Studies* 17, 133–45.

Bakvis, H. (2000). "Rebuilding Policy Capacity in the Era of the Fiscal Dividend: A Report from Canada." *Governance,* 13(1), 71–103.

British Cabinet Office (2000). Adding It Up: Improving Analysis & Modelling in Central Government.

Edwards, G. C. and Wood, B. D. (1999). "Who Influences Whom? The President, Congress, and the Media." *The American Political Science Review,* 93(2), 327–44. doi:10.2307/2585399.

European Commission (2005). Institutional Assessment and Capacity Development: Why, what and how? In Tools and Methods Series Reference Document No. 1. Belgium: European Communities.

Fukuyama, F. (2013). "What Is Governance?" *Governance,* 26(3), 347–68.

Galanti, M. T. (May 2014). "Beyond Mayors and Great Men: Effectiveness, Policy Leadership and Accountability in Italian Local Government." *Contemporary Italian Politics,* 6(2), 159–77. doi:10.1080/23248823.2014.925195.

Grindle, M. S. (2004). "Good Enough Governance: Poverty Reduction and Reform in Developing Countries." *Governance,* 17(4), 525–48.

Howlett, M. (2009a). "Government Communication as a Policy Tool: A Framework for Analysis." *Canadian Political Science Review,* 3(2), 23–37.

Howlett, M. (2009b). "Policy Analytical Capacity and Evidence-based Policy-Making: Lessons from Canada." *Canadian Public Administration,* 52(2), 153–75.

Howlett, M. and Lindquist, E. (2004). "Policy Analysis and Governance: Analytical and Policy Styles in Canada." *Journal of Comparative Policy Analysis*, 6(3), 225–49.

Klijn, E. H. and Koppenjan, J. F. M. (2000). "Interactive Decision Making and Representative Democracy: Institutional Collisions and Solutions," in Van Heffen, O., Kickert, W. J. M., and Thomassen, J. J. A. (Eds.), *Governance in Modern Society: Effects, Chang and Formation of Government Institutions*. Dordrecht: Kluwer, pp. 109–34.

Matthews, F. (2012). "Governance and State Capacity," in *The Oxford Handbook of Governance*. Oxford: Oxford University Press, p. 281.

Moon, M. Jae, Lee, Jooho, and Roh, Chul-Young (January 2014) "The Evolution of Internal IT Applications and E-Government Studies in Public Administration Research Themes and Methods." *Administration & Society*, 46(1), 3–36. doi:10.1177/0095399712459723.

Morgan, D. R. and Watson, S. S. (1992). "Policy Leadership in Council-Manager Cities: Comparing Mayor and Manager." *Public Administration Review*, 52(5), 438–46. doi:10.2307/976803.

OECD (2006). The Challenge of Capacity Development: Working Towards Good Practice. In DAC Guidelines and Reference Series. Paris: Organisation for Economic Co-operation and Development.

Oliphant, S. and Howlett. M. (2010). "Assessing Policy Analytical Capacity: Comparative Insights from a Study of the Canadian Environmental Policy Advice System." *Journal of Comparative Policy Analysis: Research and Practice*, 12(4), 439. doi:10.1080/13876988.2010.495510.

Parsons, W. (2004). "Not Just Steering but Weaving: Relevant Knowledge and the Craft of Building Policy Capacity and Coherence." *Australian Journal of Public Administration*, 63(1),43–57.

Peters, B. G. (1996). *The Policy Capacity of Government*. Ottawa: Canadian Centre for Management Development.

Peters, B. G. and Pierre, J. (2004). "Politicization of the civil service: concepts, causes, consequences," in Guy, B. and Peters, Jon Pierre (Eds.), *Politicization of the Civil Service in Comparative Perspective: The Quest for Control*. New York: Routledge, pp. 1–13.

Peters, B. G., Pierre, J., and Randma-Liiv, T. (2011). "Global Financial Crisis, Public Administration and Governance: Do New Problems Require New Solutions?" *Public Organization Review*, 11(1), 13–27.

Peters, B. G. (1998). "Managing Horizontal Government: The Politics of Co–Ordination." *Public Administration*, 76(2), 295–311.

Pierre, J. and Peters, B. G. (2000). *Governance, Politics and the State*. New York: St. Martin's Press.

Pierre, J. and Painter, M. (2005). "Unpacking policy capacity: Issues and themes," In Painter, M. and Pierre, J. (Eds.), *Challenges to State Policy Capacity: Global Trends and Comparative Perspectives*. London: Palgrave.

Radaelli, C. M. (2009). "Measuring Policy Learning: Regulatory Impact Assessment in Europe." *Journal of European Public Policy*, 16(8), 1145–64.

Radin, B. A. (June 2013)."Policy Analysis Reaches Midlife." *Central European Journal of Public Policy*, 7(1), 8–27.

Ramesh, M., Howlett, Michael P., and Saguin, Kidjie (2016). "Measuring Individual-Level Analytical, Managerial and Political Policy Capacity: A Survey Instrument." Lee Kuan Yew School of Public Policy Research Paper (16–07).

Renn, O. (1995). "Style of Using Scientific Expertise: A Comparative Framework." *Science and Public Policy*, 22(3), 147–56.

Riddell, N. (2007). "Policy Research Capacity in the Federal Government." Ottawa: Policy Research Initiative.

Salamon, L. M. (2002). *The Tools of Government: A Guide to the New Governance*. New York: Oxford University Press.

Savoia, A. and Sen, K. (2012). "Measurement and Evolution of State Capacity: Exploring a Lesser Known Aspect of Governance." *Effective States and Inclusive Development Research Centre Working Paper* 10.

Savoie, D. (2003). *Breaking the Bargain: Public Servants, Ministers and Parliament*. Toronto: University of Toronto Press.

UNDP (2010). *Measuring Capacity*. New York: United Nations Development Programme.

Varone, F., Jacob, S., and De Winter, L. (2005). "Polity, Politics and Policy Evaluation in Belgium." *Evaluation*, 11(3), 253–73.

Wallis, J. and Dollery, B. (1999). *Market Failure, Government Failure, Leadership and Public Policy*. London: St. Martin's Press.

Wallis, J. and Dollery, B. (January 2007). "Autonomous Policy Leadership: Steering a Policy Process in the Direction of a Policy Quest." *Governance*, 10(1), 1–22. doi:10.1111/0952–1895.261996026.

Wu, X., Ramesh, M., and Howlett, M. (2015). "Policy Capacity: A Conceptual Framework for Understanding Policy Competences and Capabilities." *Policy and Society*, 34(3), 165–71.

Zhang, Y. and Feiock, R. C. (April 2010). "City Managers' Policy Leadership in Council-Manager Cities." *Journal of Public Administration Research and Theory*, 20(2), 461–76. doi:10.1093/jopart/mup015.

Index